The secrets of success in marketing

How to accelerate your marketing performance

Ian Linton

Prentice Hall
Business
is an imprint of

Harlow, England • London • New York • Boston • San Francisco • Toronto
Sydney • Tokyo • Singapore • Hong Kong • Seoul • Taipei • New Delhi
Cape Town • Madrid • Mexico City • Amsterdam • Munich • Paris • Milan

PEARSON EDUCATION LIMITE

Edinburgh Gate
Harlow CM20 2JE
Tel: +44 (0)1279 623623
Fax: +44 (0)1279 431059
Website: www.pearsoned.co.uk

First published in Great Britain in 2

© Pearson Education 2011

The right of Ian Linton to be identified as author of this work has been asserted by him in accordance with the Copyright, Designs and Patents Act 1988.

Pearson Education is not responsible for the content of third party internet sites.

ISBN: 978-0-273-74244-9

British Library Cataloguing-in-Publication Data
A catalogue record for this book is available from the British Library

Library of Congress Cataloging-in-Publication Data
Linton, Ian.
The secrets of success in marketing: how to accelerate your marketing performance
/ Ian Linton.
    p. cm.
Includes index.
ISBN 978-0-273-74244-9(pbk.)
1. Marketing--Management. I. Title.
HF5415.13.L554 2011
658.8--dc22
                    2010036266

10 9 8 7 6 5 4 3 2 1
14 13 12 11 10

Typeset in 10 pt Iowan Old Style by 30
Printed and bound in Great Britain by Henry Ling Ltd, Dorchester, Dorset

Contents

About the author

IAN LINTON, a graduate of the University of Bristol, is a professional writer and marketing consultant, specialising in business-to-business communications and management books. He has more than 30 years' experience in the business and has handled a wide range of marketing and communications programmes for international clients such as AT&T, Barclays Bank, BP Chemicals, Cisco, Dell, Ernst & Young, Ford, IBM, KPMG, Office of the Deputy Prime Minister, Shell, Siemens and Vauxhall. He is the author of more than 20 business books in the fields of marketing and customer service and has written a number of case studies for the Chartered Institute of Marketing.

Introduction

IF YOU WANT TO KNOW the secrets of success in marketing, you first need to know what success means. For some people, success means making it to the top – maybe getting promotion to marketing director, or taking on a key marketing role with a famous brand. Other people measure their success by winning marketing awards or seeing their brand achieve market leadership.

Everyone working in marketing has their own view of success. It's a great career, and it can be well paid. Marketing is exciting and it can make a difference to your company's overall success. Within the broad category of marketing, your career can go in many different directions – for example, gaining promotion through the marketing management ranks, or specialising in areas as diverse as channel management, new media, market research, event coordination and customer relationship management. Marketing managers can take responsibility for individual products, brands or specific sectors. At the top of the career path, marketing directors can be appointed to the main board or move into broader executive posts, such as managing director or chief executive. Marketing isn't just restricted to careers within a company structure. You have the opportunity to work in marketing services companies, such as advertising agencies, marketing consultancies or market research organisations.

With so much diversity, it can be difficult to put your finger on what success in marketing means to you as an individual. But it's not just your own view that counts – you can't ignore the opinion of other people,

marketing activities have to make a real commercial impact

particularly those at the top. And attitudes towards marketing are changing in the difficult climate that has prevailed since the global economic crisis. The people who determine and control your marketing budgets and resources are now looking very hard at the return on marketing investment. They want to see measurable results that make a tangible difference to the company's bottom line. In other words, your marketing activities have to make a real commercial impact and that is becoming one of the most important measurements of success, particularly when other departments like sales are fighting to maintain their own share of shrinking company budgets.

On a day-to-day level, you might measure progress by something tangible like the number of leads your latest campaign generates, or the quality of visitors to an exhibition stand that you organised. Perhaps you simply would like your colleagues to say what a great campaign you ran, or to tell you that they saw your new advertisement on television last night.

Success comes in many different shapes and forms and so do the marketing solutions that can help you achieve success. That's why a book like this is so important. It highlights the broad areas where you need to focus attention – getting closer to customers, building a reputation for leadership, communicating effectively with the right decision makers, creating a great team and getting the most from your budgets.

What you'll find here is a series of ideas that you can put into practice to tackle those projects that don't appear in marketing textbooks. They're an accumulation of experience gained through working on great campaigns with companies who are leaders in their field, and they can spark ideas that you can transfer to your own markets. For example, how did a component manufacturer build one of the world's strongest brands? How did a company that gave away its services for free turn that service operation into one of its most profitable divisions? Why should you spend part of your budget on showing that your company is financially stable?

I've been involved in marketing as a campaign planner, communications consultant and business writer for over 30 years. I have worked with leading companies in technology, financial services, professional services and the automotive industry throughout that time. What I have found is that the leading companies get the basics right – focused research, advertising with impact, effective public relations – but what makes the difference is those special projects that differentiate them from competitors. The programmes that moved the reputation of a dealer network from embarrassing to one that was envied in the industry. The campaigns that helped a company quickly establish leadership in a new sector by working with the right partners. The thought-leadership programmes that transformed the image of a company in the eyes of its customers.

They're just some of the ways you can add a winning edge to your marketing. And you'll find that's essential because, with budget restrictions, you've got to keep on doing more for less and you've got to demonstrate that you are bringing real value to your business.

So, use this book as a great marketing resource. It's project based and practical. You'll find guidelines for putting ideas into practice and learn how other companies have used those ideas to gain a real edge. The book begins with the most important element in marketing – the customer relationship. Everything else hinges around that. You'll find out how to strengthen that relationship, where to focus your attention, and how to encourage other people in your company to make customers their number one priority.

Put those secrets into practice in your company and you'll become an invaluable member of the team with great career prospects.

PART 1

Closer to your customers: the true measure of success

Winning and retaining the right type of customer is the major focus of your marketing efforts. Just how do you get close to your customers, and how do you know you're targeting customers who will prove profitable in the long term? This section looks at some of the techniques for building relationships that pay.

1 Get up close and personal with the precision of one-to-one marketing

The concept of personalised products and services for individual customers is a reality in many sectors. When you can learn so much about customers from the information they volunteer, why compromise on 'vanilla' campaigns?

2 A lifetime together – the true value of long-term customer relationships

It's common knowledge that it costs more to win new customers than retain existing ones. A measure called 'lifetime customer value' can help you identify the customers you really want to keep. It compares the cost of acquiring individual customers with their purchase history and their account management costs. Information like this highlights who should stay and who should go from your customer base.

3 Community service – a problem shared

These days, companies positively welcome complaints and suggestions. By encouraging feedback and responding to it, you can learn far more about what your customers really think about your products – and demonstrate that you are doing something about it. By allowing customers to share that knowledge online, you can build a community and get new, sometimes unexpected allies, in the form of people who want to solve problems for each other.

4 Put customers on your product development team

Your customers can make an important contribution to your new product programme, either through recommendations on direction, features and performance, or through evaluation. Either way, their contribution can ensure that your new products meet real market needs and the process also helps to strengthen customer relationships.

5 Pass the parcel – make it easier for customers to contact you

Do your customers have to find their way through a maze of different phone numbers to get an answer? Do they get passed from extension to extension once they're through? More importantly, do the people answering the customer calls have access to all customer records, purchase history, emails, service requests and complaints? A single point of contact and an integrated customer record can make it easier to deal with every customer contact effectively.

1

Get up close and personal with the precision of one-to-one marketing

READ ANY MARKETING BOOK and you'll find that the emphasis is firmly on customers – who they are, what they want, how you can meet their real needs. Go back a few decades and customers were a pretty amorphous bunch. Mass markets were the 'nirvana' for high-volume manufacturers, so detailed customer knowledge wasn't a priority. Today, the contact between buyer and seller on the Internet is moving towards the ultimate one-to-one experience. Database technology supports a level of personalisation that can deliver highly tailored products and services to specific individuals. Each time a customer logs on to a website, for example, the database can pull together purchase history and personal preferences as a basis for a highly personalised response. By giving customers a single point of entry, you can increase customer loyalty and learn more about their purchasing patterns. This provides an excellent basis for adding value and for the development of new products.

Marketing secret

◆ When you can learn so much about customers from the information they volunteer, why compromise on 'vanilla' campaigns?

Building one-to-one relationships involves collecting and using information about actual and prospective customers as a basis for a customised selling approach. This provides an efficient and targeted means of maximising sales. For one-to-one marketing to work effectively, you need the right level of information on customers. You may not always be able to get that level of information on individual customers. However, if you have sufficient information on groups of customers with common needs, you can use techniques such as direct mail to communicate with a degree of precision. As your information on individual customers grows, you can move towards one-to-one communication.

One-to-one marketing is designed to:

◆ improve the quality of customer service

◆ strengthen customer relationships

◆ maximise the profitability of each customer relationship

◆ increase retention rates for customers

◆ maximise the return on your investment in marketing and customer service.

One-to-one marketing cannot guarantee loyalty, but it can make an important contribution. Customers will remain only if they continue to recognise the value of your products and the quality of your customer service. That means continually enhancing the customer experience.

Refine your target market

The more information you have about your target audience, the more precise you can make your campaign. In an ideal world, direct marketing techniques would allow you to communicate one-to-one with every prospect, but in practical terms you are more likely to be communicating with groups who share the same characteristics. This enables you to develop a unique relationship that competitors will find very difficult to match. It can also reduce your marketing and customer management costs by reducing wastage to a minimum.

At the heart of effective one-to-one marketing is a data networking solution that collects, stores, manages, and distributes all relevant customer information via a single, integrated customer database. The database is updated from all customer channels and should be accessible by all customer-facing staff.

Marketing secret

◆ Personalisation develops a unique customer relationship that competitors will find very difficult to match.

The more you know about your customers, the better your chances of increasing their value to your company. Data capture must therefore be an integral part of all your sales, marketing, and customer service campaigns. You can

find out more about your customers

build detailed profiles through campaign responses and customer research, and use the latest database and communications technology to manage, analyse, and distribute information. Take every opportunity to find out more about your customers so that you can build a real competitive edge, based on one-to-one personal relationships.

The rapid development of data storage and data analysis tools means that it is now possible to know far more about your customers – with information well beyond details of income, spending patterns, service preferences, and frequency of use. The information available represents a quantum leap in the ability to profile customers.

Developing personalised welcome pages

A key element of the one-to-one relationship is the personalised welcome page on your website. This is a modified home page with personalised messages triggered by identification of a customer and it can boost online revenue as well as reinforcing the relationship. Commentators have identified two types of personalisation – 'implicit' and 'explicit':

◆ Implicit user profiles are created from user behaviour or from user information that can be automatically identified, such as IP address or browser information. The most common form of implicit personalisation is based on the history of a user's clicks or pages they have recently viewed to personalise future content.

◆ Explicit user profiles are created when a user registers with a site. The details that the user enters during registration are used to personalise content on a site.

The welcome page uses intelligence in a database to precisely tailor marketing programmes to individual customers. It offers recommendations to customers based on their purchase history and previous searches, and reminds customers of their recent searches on site. The page can also include special offers based on the value of customer or their frequency of purchase and may feature fast-track buying mechanisms, like Amazon's '1-click' with customer details preloaded. For new visitors, it can display messages such as 'Customers who bought ... also bought ... and ...' to encourage browsing.

Marketing secret
◆ A personalised welcome page allows greater interaction with customers and increases revenue.

Personalising a website landing page brings many important benefits, including:

◆ more efficient conversion of visitors into customers

◆ increased profit from advertising investments

◆ improved customer satisfaction

◆ higher rate of repeat visits

◆ increased revenue and enhanced profitability from higher purchasing levels

◆ deeper insight into customer behaviour.

Use information carefully

If you offer personal pages on your website, you can allow customers to add further choices to the profile, using a special checklist. However, it is important to use customer information in appropriate ways. Attempts to increase customer interactions and to provide more personalised information have made many consumers concerned about privacy issues. Critics of personalised welcome pages believe that some consumers are suspicious of websites that try to extract information from them. They claim that these consumers avoid website personalisation because of concerns that marketers would misuse the information. It is therefore essential to let customers control the frequency and scope of interaction.

use customer information in appropriate ways

Marketing secret

◆ Customers are willing to provide information only when they see real benefits.

Information should be used to meet individual customer needs. Customers are aware of the value of their information and are willing to provide it only when they see real benefits. That means giving customers control over their data and the way they interact with your company. To build trust, you must allow customers to choose how they want to interact and to control what information they provide. Once you have customer information, it is important to act on it. Make sure that you maintain regular contact by sending customers information or special offers tailored to their individual needs.

Website software can be used to automatically personalise the contents on your home page as soon as a visitor arrives. Use phrases that have been proven to work, such as:

◆ Others who searched for ... usually liked ...

◆ People who bought this item also bought ...

◆ Other users suggest you refine your search like this ...

◆ Welcome back! Based on your history with us, we think you will like ...

◆ Welcome! Those who came from ... searching for ... usually bought ...

◆ Thanks for your recent order. People who bought what you ordered usually added ...

◆ Our user community thought you might like to come back to look at ...

You can use the information in your profiles to generate recommendations for the products that are most relevant for each customer. As well as increasing direct sales, this approach also results in an increase in the number of clicks per visit so that the visitor stays longer and sees more relevant products. In the longer term, this can improve customer loyalty and frequency of return visits.

the visitor stays longer and sees more relevant products

Rather than simply basing personalised offers on an individual's purchase and browsing history, you can also factor in demographic classifications as well. Offers will begin to change from 'People who bought … also bought …' to 'People like you who bought … also bought …'. This can lead to far more sophisticated and specific marketing activities, with multiple personalised campaigns for each of your products or services. Factors such as the shopper's location, age, sex and occupation can be used to determine the way they are targeted and the offers they receive.

This type of information also allows you to offer different levels of service to each category of customer. These could include:

◆ privileged rewards for top customers

◆ incentives for regular customers to spend more

◆ special offers to lapsed customers.

Help customers help themselves

Interactive facilities on a website allow customers to design their own customised products. Cars and computers are good examples. The customer chooses a basic model, and then selects features and options from a database. The system provides a price for the customised product, then gives the customer the choice of ordering now or storing the specification on a personal web page for later modification. The high level of interaction gives customers greater choice and provides you with detailed insight into their needs.

Marketing secret

◆ Interactive facilities provide you with great insight into customer behaviour.

You can also use data on customer preferences as a basis for offering personalised information services. Customers specify the type of information they need, and they are alerted by email whenever relevant information is available.

Trends indicate that consumer trust in advertisements is declining, with more attention paid to recommendations and advice from friends and other consumers. One study reported that almost 80 per cent of European consumers who regularly use the Internet trust recommendations from family and friends, and almost 40 per cent trust recommendations from anonymous online sources. The same survey reported that, before making their purchases, more than 20 per cent of online purchasers were consulting comparison sites or community pages where other consumers write about their experiences with products and the companies that supply them.

You can build trust and encourage stronger commitment from your customers by enabling them to communicate their opinions, write reviews and create their own personal lists on your site. You can also inform your customers about other customers who have the same needs and preferences, describing the products they bought, the reviews that they wrote, and other observations.

Marketing secret

◆ To increase the benefits of personalisation further, encourage customers to make and share recommendations.

A growing number of websites feature simplified purchasing systems that allow pre-registered customers to bypass a conventional shopping cart and online checkout by purchasing a product with a single mouse click. The enabler is a cookie that allows the web server to recognise the purchaser and relate their order to specific credit and shipping information previously submitted by the purchaser and stored on the server. This adds even further value to the personalised welcome page, as well as reducing the risk of abandoned purchases.

Gain insight from every customer contact

To enhance customer service, increase revenue and strengthen customer loyalty, it's essential to capture customer insight from every form of customer contact. In a retail or online environment, where there is a recognisable transaction point, such as the checkout, it is relatively straightforward to collect customer data that enables real insight to be developed. However, for many organisations with multiple customer interaction points, this can be more difficult because there is no single point-of-sale transaction history or web log to analyse. The challenge is how to capture that essential data, extract customer insight and build a total picture of customer engagements as a basis for delivering targeted messages and offers, thus enhancing customer loyalty and maximising lifetime customer revenue. Smartcards provide a way of achieving that.

Smartcards provide the card issuer with valuable information about customers and their behaviour with the card. When the customer uses the card to access an area, such as an entertainment venue, or make a purchase, the 'transaction' is recorded. The data from all transactions builds individual customer profiles, showing how often a customer visits, which areas they access and which goods or services they purchase electronically with their card.

Marketing secret

◆ Capturing data from every customer transaction helps to build a complete picture of customer behaviour.

Managing multiple customer interaction points and taking advantage of the data available from them is a major factor in achieving closer relationships with customers. Customer data from many different sources can build up an entire picture of customer interactions. This represents an important opportunity to understand current and future customer value. To grow business, organisations have to know much more about their customers by using appropriate technology to analyse their activities and trigger appropriate responses and actions. The aim is to gain deeper understanding by knowing what your visitors are doing, what they spend, how often they visit an outlet and what they prefer.

As an example, a growing number of entertainment venues are eliminating individual paper tickets and issuing customers with smartcards that enable them to learn more about customers' behaviour and buying patterns. Members with smartcards will have the convenience of e-ticketing, privileged access to VIP areas and some cashless purchasing.

The venue owners can also find out how visitors are consuming multiple services: for example, a meal with an event, or a drink after an event. This will enable them to market multiple services more effectively.

The detailed information available from smartcards enables the venue to communicate and interact effectively with customers through personalised messages and offers. It can also be used as a basis for making targeted offers to individual customers based on their past behaviour or the behaviour of similar groups. This, in turn, can help to build and strengthen customer loyalty, increasing long-term revenue and profitability. The information also proves valuable in identifying products or services that are popular or are underused.

Use data to improve marketing precision

The challenge is to turn occasional customers into enthusiastic regular customers by enhancing the whole buying experience. In a venue, a smartcard, combined with an electronic purse facility, can be used to improve convenience and create a seamless experience for customers by providing them with a single token of identity and payment mechanism for all the facilities at a venue, such as parking, event tickets, merchandise and refreshments. Data can also be used to enhance products and services that recognise the individual needs of customers and develop customised offers.

Information from smartcards can be used to create multi-level loyalty programmes tailored to individual customer profiles. In a venue, the programmes can feature added-value services, such as delivery from virtual kiosks that enable

> **Marketing secret**
>
> ◆ Customer insight makes it easier to target marketing
>   more precisely with customised offers and one-to-one
>   communications.

visitors to pre-order merchandise away from crowds at the
main kiosk or to pre-order through a personalised web portal.
Although smartcards provide valuable data,
it's essential to utilise data to meet business
objectives, and not gather it for its own sake.
Organisations must be clear about what
the business output will be. Data gathering
should be driven by marketing needs – how

*data gathering
should be driven by
marketing needs*

we can market more products or fill a venue, how we can
communicate more precisely with customers. Start by identifying what kind of customer insight can be achieved, and how
the data can be used to get the best results for customers.

Once that insight is in place, it becomes possible to target
marketing more precisely, but it doesn't have to be complicated. The marketing programme can be simple in the
early stages: for example, sending an email 24 hours before
an event telling customers that you are looking forward to
seeing them, and following up after the event, saying that
you hope they enjoyed the event and asking for feedback.
Doing simple things like this can make a real difference.

Using intelligence to shape individual customer responses
creates even greater revenue opportunities with high value-
visitors. An example is a pay-as-you-drive insurance service
that employs existing technology such as satellite navigation

linked to smartcards to create an innovative model that tracks customers' cars and charges them according to where they drive. This breaks the mould of driver's insurance and enables insurers to reach marginalised markets, such as people who don't drive very far in a year. This insight adds value, improving service to customers even further.

Personally speaking

The concept of personalised products and services for individual customers is a reality in many sectors. That makes a powerful contribution to customer loyalty and it also gives smaller agile companies the chance to compete effectively with larger organisations by focusing on niche markets. Add the facilities of short-run manufacturing, perhaps through a partner, and you have a recipe for success that benefits both customer and supplier.

The ability to be selective about your customers becomes even more important when you are looking at issues like profitability. As the next chapter shows, not all customers are equal, so it's important to make use of a measure called 'lifetime customer value' that can help you identify the customers you really want to keep.

2

A lifetime together – the true value of long-term customer relationships

IT'S COMMON KNOWLEDGE that it costs more to win new customers than retain existing ones. Customer acquisition should never be neglected, because exist-

ing business may decline for reasons outside your control. However, industry experience indicates that existing customers make a comparatively greater contribution when marketing costs are taken into considera-

identify the customers you really want to keep

tion. A measure called 'lifetime customer value' can help you identify the customers you really want to keep by comparing the cost of acquiring and managing individual customers with their purchase history.

Lifetime customer value is a way of measuring how much your customers are worth over the time they are buying from you. Long-term customers can increase sales and profits significantly, so it is important to retain customers, but not at the cost of other essential marketing activities. For example, your customer base could prove to be too large if retention costs are high. Those costs include sales visits, telephone contact and marketing collateral. Using lifetime customer value, you can calculate the cost and contribution of each customer, and decide the optimum level of business.

Marketing secret

◆ Not all customers are valuable. Measuring lifetime value will demonstrate their true contribution to your business.

Customer loyalty programmes, although they appear to be similar, are designed to retain as many customers as possible, regardless of their real value. The lifetime customer value calculation indicates the contribution individual customers make to profitability. This can provide the basis for retention programmes that are more carefully targeted.

Apply the lifetime customer value concept

The lifetime for customers will vary from industry to industry, and from brand to brand, sometimes within a single company. The lifetime of customers comes to an end when their contribution becomes so small as to be insignificant, unless steps are taken to revitalise them. Although it is important to retain customers, there are two important questions:

1   Is it really sensible to keep as many customers as possible?

2   Should retention activities take precedence over customer acquisition programmes?

Industry experience indicates that a number of benefits apply:

◆ A 5 per cent increase in customer retention can create a 125 per cent increase in profits.

◆ A 10 per cent increase in retailer retention can translate to a 20 per cent increase in sales.

◆ Extending customer life cycles by three years can treble profits per customer.

Before calculating lifetime customer value, it is important to break your customers down into four key categories. This can help to clarify analysis and act as the basis for marketing activities to improve lifetime customer value:

◆ A good customer is a long-term customer who regularly buys a profitable product, and who has bought recently.

◆ A new customer may be the best customer of all, since their lifetime value has yet to be realised.

◆ A long-term customer who does not buy regularly, and has not bought recently, is probably not a customer at all.

◆ A lapsed customer who has been re-recruited often behaves like a new customer.

If you market to consumers, lifetime customer value is calculated by analysing the behaviour of a group of customers who have the same recruitment date. The group could consist of:

◆ Specific types of customers (for example, in the same socio-economic group).

◆ Customers recruited from the same source.

◆ Customers who bought the same types of product.

If you operate in a business-to-business environment, you can use a similar approach but consider additional sector-specific factors:

◆ Isolate particular customers, and examine them individually.

◆ Analyse the behaviour of different groups, segmenting your customer database by factors such as industry, annual turnover or staff numbers.

The calculation

The basic calculation has three stages:

1 Identify a discrete group of customers for tracking.

2 Record (or estimate) revenue and cost for each group of customers by campaign or time period.

3 Calculate the contribution by campaign or time period.

Other factors can be introduced to make the calculation more relevant. In a business-to-business environment, for example, it may be your sales representatives who generate sales. In this case, the calculation should include the representative's 'running costs' and the cost of any centrally-produced sales support material.

The table below shows the calculations for a sample group of customers who were recruited through a direct response advertising campaign that ran in the spring of Year 1. The table tracks their expenditure over a 5-year period.

TABLE 2.1 *Calculating customer value*

Campaign	Total customer expenditure	Total marketing costs	Total contribution
Spring Year 1	£50,000	£45,000	£5,000
Total Year 1	£75,000	£60,000	£15,000
Total Year 2	£85,000	£65,000	£20,000
Total Year 3	£92,000	£68,500	£23,500
Total Year 4	£107,000	£81,000	£26,000
Total Year 5	£115,000	£86,000	£29,000
Overall total	£524,000	£405,500	£118,500

Divide the total contribution by the number of customers in the group. Say there are 1,000 customers: the average lifetime value per customer is £1,185.

Your company may offer different products or brands, which are marketed under different cost centres. If a customer deals with more than one cost/profit centre, there is a choice of approaches:

◆ Examine customers of each brand and ignore multiple purchases.

◆ Build a more detailed model that combines and allocates the cumulative costs as well as the cumulative profit in the appropriate proportions.

Use lifetime customer values to improve marketing performance

There are four important applications:

◆ Set target customer acquisition costs.

◆ Allocate acquisition funds.

◆ Select acquisition offers.

◆ Support customer retention activities.

Marketing secret

◆ Understanding lifetime customer value can help you budget more accurately for customer acquisition programmes.

Set target customer acquisition costs

If a customer is expected to generate more than one sale, the allowable acquisition cost can be greater than the cost allowed for the first sale – the classic loss-leader approach. However, overspending on customer acquisition can also be risky. A reasonable calculation is to recruit only from those sources that yield new customers at less than half the estimated lifetime value. On that basis, the worst sources will have a cost per customer close to a lifetime value, while the average cost per customer should be far lower.

Allocate acquisition funds

Different recruitment sources will provide customers with different lifetime values. After identifying those values, spend more on the best sources. Lifetime value also can be applied when allocating funds between customer acquisition and revival of lapsed customers.

Select acquisition offers

The lifetime value of a customer may depend on the type and value of their initial purchase. This can help you decide which products and offers to use or whether to upgrade or downgrade existing customers.

Support customer retention activities

Once the typical lifetime value of a group of customers is known, you can decide how hard to work at retaining them. Activities should be tailored to the customers who are most valuable.

Increase value with new offers

Lifetime customer value analysis reinforces a traditional marketing rule of thumb, that it costs less to retain existing customers than to acquire new ones. Overemphasis on new business development could be a bad move. However, customer retention costs money in terms of sales and marketing funds and lifetime customer value analysis indicates that not all customers are worth retaining. You should carefully select the customers who are likely to yield the highest returns over a period of time. When you have identified the most valuable customers, you need to have a wide range of products or services to offer them. Cross-selling and up-selling are the best ways to increase lifetime customer value, but this can be difficult with a limited product range.

it costs less to retain existing customers

As an example, a financial services company can increase lifetime customer value by cross-selling a range of different products and services such as:

◆ current account

◆ personal loans

◆ life assurance

◆ investment advice

◆ savings account

◆ mortgage

◆ pension

◆ taxation services.

Focus on profitability

Increasing customer profitability can be a tricky process. You may have offered customers discounts or free services in the past to win or retain business. If the cost of providing those services or discounts exceeds customer profitability, you have to decide on the difficult strategy of cutting costs or losing customers. Trying to win new business can be stressful, expensive and often unrewarding. Your resources would be better spent on improving profitability from existing customer relationships. As the cost of acquiring new customers increases, your acquisition efforts must focus on those customers with the highest potential to become profitable. Industry statistics indicate that keeping existing customers costs less than acquiring new ones:

◆ Acquiring a customer costs 5 to 10 times more than retaining one.

◆ A 5 per cent increase in retention yields profit increases of 25 to 100 per cent.

◆ Repeat customers spend, on average, 67 per cent more.

◆ 20 per cent of customers account for 80 per cent of total revenues.

Retention is about more than keeping customers; it's also about maintaining their value. Although customer retention is critical, it's important to recognise that not all existing customers may be profitable. Historic sales policies may have created a situation in which profitability varies by customer or even by transaction. Profitability can be influenced by different types of discounts, penalties, allowances as well as rebates in kind, or additional services given for free. It can be easy to lose control of these factors as your business, product range and customer base has grown. An ad-hoc approach means that mistakes may pass unnoticed, discounts are no longer calculated on any logical scale and additional services are distributed over-generously. As a result profitability levels may be compromised.

Marketing secret

◆ Customer retention programmes should concentrate on maximising value, not retaining customers for their own sake.

On the other hand, what do you do if you have an incomplete view of customer value and profitability? With fragmented customer data, it can be difficult to consolidate varied data from internal and external systems into one place. That makes it difficult to predict customer behaviour or measure the success of marketing campaigns or customer initiatives. Software is available to help you assess customer profitability by accurately analysing revenue, direct costs and indirect costs for individual customers and market sectors based on the transactions of those customers and the services that they consume. The software delivers a number of important benefits:

◆ Identifies the profitability of individual customers and their profit drivers.

◆ Provides information to determine the processes that are driving customer profits.

◆ Delivers profitability reports that underpin marketing, sales, channel and customer retention decisions.

◆ Provides income and cost reports for individual customers to support customer negotiations on terms such as number of deliveries, minimum order sizes, returns, payment terms and services.

Build a long-term picture of the customer

An ideal strategy is to expand your pool of profitable customers, with the ultimate goal of optimising each customer's lifetime value. However, it can be difficult to match compelling offers with the right customers at the right time.

Customers may buy products and services via a number of different channels, and they may have several accounts. Disparate customer databases also make it difficult

expand your pool of profitable customers

to construct a consolidated view of each customer. Without a complete view of the customer and an understanding of which customers are profitable and why, it's impossible to determine which types of customers you should acquire and which ones you should seek to retain. The key to improved customer acquisition and retention is gathering and analysing all your customer data in order to understand customer behaviour and develop more effective marketing strategies.

A key factor in analysing customer profitability is the cost of serving individual customers. Customers fall into two main categories:

1   High cost-to-serve customers.

2   Low cost-to-serve customers.

The customer characteristics that influence cost-to-serve include:

◆ order custom products or standard products

◆ small order quantities or high order quantities

◆ unpredictable order arrivals or predictable order arrivals

◆ require customised delivery or standard delivery

◆ frequently change delivery requirements

◆ require large amounts of pre-sales support (marketing, technical and sales resources) or little to no pre-sales support (standard pricing and ordering)

◆ require large amounts of post-sales support (installation, training, warranty and field service) or no post-sales support

◆ require company to hold inventory

◆ pay slowly or pay on time.

As customer demands for higher and higher levels of service increase, there are two possible outcomes. First, you could incur large losses in serving those customers that demand large quantities of these special services. Or, second, to avoid the losses, you may decide not to supply the services requested by your customers. By identifying the true cost of delivering service, you will have a firm basis for adjusting prices or levels of service to improve profitability.

Marketing secret

◆ Measuring the cost of serving customers is a critical stage in building profitability.

You may be able to deal with customer demands by improving your own supply process and reducing cost-to-serve levels. If, for example, customers are moving to smaller order sizes, you should look at your order handling processes, so that you can accommodate customer preferences at lower cost without raising overall prices. Electronic systems, for example, can lower the cost of processing large quantities of small orders. If customers like product variety, you could

if customers like product variety, you could introduce modular designs

introduce modular designs so that you can offer greater variety and customisation without cost penalties.

Customised or menu pricing policies should be at the heart of any strategy to manage customer profitability. By understanding the true cost of providing services, you can establish prices that transform unprofitable relationships into profitable ones. You can set the prices of special services to recover the cost of providing them and allow the customer to choose the menu of services they prefer. Pricing policies in this way educates customers about costs and can help to improve relationships. Activity-based pricing enables you to lower the cost of serving customers. You may also be able to gain additional market share by offering lower prices to customers who want only a basic level of services.

transform unprofitable relationships into profitable ones

Concentrate on the best customers

Given the variable costs of service, it's important to concentrate on keeping and rewarding the most profitable and regular customers at the expense of others. Some companies take this a stage further and fire their worst customers. That can influence the direction of marketing strategy. Instead of advertising to attract new customers with special offers, those companies focus on loyalty programmes to retain the small proportion of their customer base that provides the highest per centage of profits.

Programmes such as these don't just help you hold onto customers, they can also shape the services you offer customers. Using data from loyalty programmes, you can offer differentiated products and services based on customer preferences. A simple example would be customer mailings offering different discounts and offers based on individual spending levels.

> *Marketing secret*
>
> ◆ Differentiating service is an important tool for retaining the most profitable customers.

The starting point for differentiated service is to profile your best customers. Your sales records can provide insight but, if you lack a comprehensive view of the customer, ask them directly for the information you need using surveys and feedback. This can help to make customers feel appreciated and increase their loyalty. Your top customers are likely to buy more frequently, spend more money, cost less per sale and refer others. This can make an important contribution to profitability.

The key message is, don't overspend to attract new business in the short term. Operate focused customer acquisition programmes to win new customers but, once they are on board, drive additional sales and build relationships by treating every customer as your best customer. That way you won't have to keep spending 5 to 10 times more to bring in new customers. A fraction of that investment can keep customers coming back repeatedly.

The bottom line

As we saw in the opening chapter, high-volume mass marketing is no longer the holy grail. These days the focus is on profitable business and that begins with profitable customers. 'Some you win, some you lose' is a good attitude to take, particularly when it comes to identifying the customers who really matter. Calculating lifetime customer value is an important measure for building profitable business and focusing your marketing budget on the most profitable customers. With tightening budgets and a demand for better bottom line performance, it's really important to do more for less and use your resources to retain the best customers.

The good news is that building strong customer relationships doesn't depend just on marketing spend. As the next chapter shows, encouraging community among customers can generate high levels of loyalty.

3

Community service
– a problem shared

THESE DAYS, COMPANIES positively welcome complaints and suggestions. By encouraging feedback and responding to it, you can learn far more about what your customers really think about your products – and demonstrate that you are doing something about it. By allowing customers to share that knowledge online, you can build a community and get new, sometimes unexpected allies, in the form of people who want to solve problems for each other. Communications technology has made it possible for both consumers and businesses to express themselves more easily and share their content and views with friends, colleagues and a wider audience. People no longer feel the need to be anonymous. Businesses now recognise the value of consumer and employee expression through blogs and other media, and have moved from a state of paranoia to active encouragement.

Get real world research

So what does this mean for your business? 'Listening in' on social networking sites can be a great way to find out more

share advice and experience

about your customers' genuine likes and dislikes. You can create greater customer interaction on your own website by encouraging customers and employees to contribute to online product reviews or by setting up customer forums to share advice and experience. These facilities can often give you a clearer picture of customer views and issues than conventional market research studies.

> *Marketing secret*
>
> ◆ By listening in on social networks you can extend the reach of your market research and get a clear picture of customer attitudes.

Commentators believe that the ability to communicate easily has created new, closer relationships between customers, suppliers, business partners and other stakeholders as all parties recognise the value and benefits of expressing views and sharing knowledge and experience. So it's a good move to positively encourage the development of content from customers, consumer groups, journalists, suppliers, business partners, consultancies, industry associations and independent research organisations, as well as from your own employees. This will give you a broader view of opinion about your products and your company, and will create a greater sense of community.

Allow customers to publish content

An important starting point is the product section of your website. Product pages should include an area for customers to post their own comments or reviews of the product. This can take the form of written comments or ratings, such as star ratings. These reviews can help to build trust, even if some of the comments are unfavourable. Critical comments may highlight problems that you were not aware of and this can make a useful contribution to a product development programme. You can go further and give customers the option of creating and displaying all their favourite product catalogues on a single site. Customers will be able to add their own descriptions and comments, giving you access to personalised information that can drive cross-sell and up-sell opportunities. An example is the 'customers' favourites' lists published on sites like Amazon.

Marketing secret

◆ Customer reviews can highlight issues that you may not have been aware of.

As well as product pages, you could also set up an online forum using commercial software. This can serve as an extension of good customer service as well as a low cost way to drive sales. Commentators believe that forums can help to build trust in both the product and the supplier, helping to develop an effective

build trust in both the product and the supplier

relationship with customers. Forums can be used to share advice about products, as well as resolving problems and airing product issues.

Although it is relatively simple to set up a forum, encouraging participation may be more difficult. Some companies offer customers incentives to participate. As an example, one company offered customers gift certificates for their first 10 posts, with a higher-value gift certificate for 250 additional posts. However, the incentives can help to pay for themselves because the average customer cashing them in is likely to spend significantly more than the value of the incentive on the company's products.

Experience indicates that companies who operate forums should keep moderation light rather than censor content, unless the material is inappropriate or defamatory. Even if customers write about a rival business and its products, don't remove the post. This indicates that the forum is open and honest and also provides valuable insight into views of competitive products. Some companies add their own comments on competitive posts, offering to match deals or give discounts on pricing or delivery.

Forums give customers the opportunity to complain about problems. However, it's essential to respond to any issues immediately. Being proactive demonstrates a concern for customer service and encourages dialogue. Solving problems can help to increase customer satisfaction and loyalty; ignoring them will discourage customers from using the forum and may lead to customer defection.

> *Marketing secret*
>
> ◆ Responding proactively to forum concerns demonstrates customer care and builds dialogue.

The biggest misconception about using social media tools is that the legal department will try to censor content or that people will say negative things about their brands. The reality is that customers in the marketplace are already saying good and bad things about brands. There is more value in finding out what's being said, addressing the issues and developing relationships. Forums and other social media give you a powerful communications channel to connect with your customers on a personal

you can create genuine goodwill

level, build trust, collect valuable feedback and strengthen relationships. By providing your audience with useful content in the form of information, help, discussion and ideas, you can create genuine goodwill. In addition, if you can draw on your customers' knowledge and ideas, you will find it easier to meet their real requirements. Listening to customers and acting on their suggestions is one of the best ways to build a community of customers who are willing to express their goodwill to other customers and prospects. That goodwill can turn into positive marketing and sales returns.

Create an informal innovation network

You can add weight to your product development programme by harnessing the growing trend of informal collaboration and expression in the workplace, encouraging employees to communicate their creative thoughts through blogs and other media. Informal networks like this can create company-wide 'thinktanks' and encourage an innovation culture. By encouraging and recognising creativity and collaboration, you can create an innovation network that extends throughout the organisation. It's important to recognise that innovation sources don't have to stop at your own boundaries. By encouraging a sense of community on your website, you can capture the knowledge and expertise of contributors inside and outside the company. The concept of external 'innovation partners' who contribute knowledge that is managed by internal staff to develop new solutions can add real value to your own research and development resources, accelerating your ability to innovate.

Marketing secret

◆ A forum can encourage experts to contribute problem-solving knowledge and help to create an informal 'innovation network'.

Such external innovation networks could incorporate contributors from suppliers, business partners, consultancies, industry associations and independent research organisations. Customers should also form an important part of the innovation process. They may have discovered new ways to use an existing product or encountered problems that you may be unaware of. An innovation network should therefore incorporate ways to involve customers in the development or customisation of their own products or services – a topic that we discuss in more detail in the next chapter.

Help customers to help each other

One of the surprising results of community growth is how willing customers can be to help each other. This has proved a major benefit for companies who need to provide their customers with high levels of technical support – customers become virtual members of the support team. When the customers post technical queries on a forum, most of the answers and suggestions come not from the company's technical staff, but from other customers. In many cases, there is almost an element of competition to see who can first come up with the right solution.

customers become virtual members of the support team

> *Marketing secret*
> ◆ Self-help facilities on your website increase your own support resources at no additional cost because your customers help each other.

This has a significant effect on the quality of customer service, by extending the range of expertise available and reducing internal support costs. It also provides good insight into customer issues and can provide valuable feedback for future product development. If you are developing this kind of support forum, make sure you capture the important solutions and build them into a support database that is open to all customers. The impact on customer satisfaction can be quite significant.

Get closer to customers with a 'collegiate environment'

A 'collegiate environment' is a good example of the way in which lines between companies and their customers are increasingly blurred, whereby customers interact and participate in product development and other processes. Conferences, workshops, collaborative working and joint development projects, as well as interactive online services, all help to contribute to the collegiate environment. The collegiate environment is an approach to customer relationships that encourages friendly cooperation and involvement, rather than the traditional supplier/buyer relationship. Informal collaboration may result from a collegiate environment, while full collaboration is a more formal relationship that will be covered by contractual agreements.

Building a collegiate environment can help position your company as an influential, trusted resource. Your marketing communications will work from a solid base of experience and expertise because you have earned the trust and respect of industry colleagues and customers. You can speak as an industry leader with a bright, concise collegial tone, and you can involve and empower your target audience. You can understand their preoccupations and priorities and you can help them see how they might relate to your company and its activities.

position your company as an influential, trusted resource

> *Marketing secret*
> ◆ A simple thing like tone of the language used can help to
>   create a sense of community.

The language you use should create a sense of partnership
and camaraderie with your audience. Your copy should
speak in a conversational tone, addressing your audience
directly, and speaking on their level, always keeping your
audience's interests and priorities in mind. The conversational tone conveys partnership and helps your audience
understand you clearly.

To build a collegiate environment, you need to communicate in the same confident way with decision makers
at every level by adapting the messages to individual needs
and concerns:

◆ **Senior executives** – The message to senior executives
   is that, through the collegiate environment you
   are creating, you can enable them and their staff to
   collaborate informally and network with top industry
   experts as well as their peers to find new solutions to the
   most important issues their company faces.

◆ **Mid-level managers** – Managers should understand
   that, by getting involved with your company, they will
   have access to the latest information and resources they
   need to tackle the technical and business challenges they
   face. They will learn about the latest products, discover
   the best solutions, share experience with other helpful
   colleagues, and hear from other innovators.

◆ **Technical staff** – A collegiate environment can help technical staff transform their own products and solutions. They will have an opportunity to learn about new approaches, read case studies and get advice from experts, giving them knowledge and inspiration they can put to practical use.

Bring customers together

A collegiate environment is particularly appropriate for conferences, workshops and other customer events. If you created the ideal conference, it would have the feel of a reunion, characterised by a sense of involvement and of being among friends. The event would be productive and collaborative, with shared information and input from people who are glad to be participating, and who enjoy working together. The conference should present delegates with the latest products, identify the most important issues, provide ample networking opportunities and feature a high level of interactive participation.

You can increase involvement by introducing events to your conference that feature your delegates. An example might be an innovation showcase in which delegates can present projects that they have worked on, with a panel of judges selecting the best entries for an innovation award. Competitions in which delegates take on relevant technical or business challenges can also encourage involvement.

Extend the collegiate environment

You can extend the collegiate environment by setting up a virtual community on the Internet to support interaction between people with a common interest. Facilities to support the community could include newsletters, discussion groups and information. You can also use your online community facilities to allow members to join an online club and enjoy privileged services, using the membership database to offer personalised incentives and promotions.

Marketing secret

◆ Extend the sense of community by offering privileges to customers who make an important contribution to the process.

An online discussion group gives users the ability to post messages on your site. The messages should represent helpful information and may include requests for help or further information. Some sites set up facilities for feedback or product review, introducing *discussion groups* an opportunity for objective, independent *help to build* comment. The aim is to encourage other *credibility* members of the community to suggest answers, provide help or contribute to the discussion of a specific issue. Discussion groups help to build credibility for the site and strengthen the relationships that are essential to the collegiate environment.

You can encourage good contributions by recognising and highlighting the best your community has to offer. This can be especially useful if your community is growing and you want to keep members involved. A 'Hall of Fame' that presents examples of the best contributions can encourage wider participation. You can enhance the collegiate atmosphere by allowing the members to pick their own favourites.

All together now

Creating a community takes time. It does not happen at one conference or through a single visit to an online community. All of your marketing communications should help to build the environment with language that is friendly and welcoming and content that empowers your customers.

Community has proved to be a powerful tool in building and strengthening customer relationships. You can take the process even further by bringing customers into your product development team, directly or indirectly, as the next chapter explains.

4

Put customers on your product development team

YOUR CUSTOMERS CAN MAKE an important contribution to your new product programme, either through recommendations on direction, features and performance, or through evaluation. Either way, their contribution can ensure that your new products meet real market needs. Involving customers in new product development can result in more targeted products with a greater chance of success, while at the same time strengthening relationships and creating mutual benefits. Customers can also make an indirect contribution when they use an online build-to-order system (such as the Dell personal computer model where customers effectively 'build' their own model). Allowing customers to configure existing products gives valuable insight into real needs and preferences – information that can feed into future development programmes.

Involve customers at an early stage

If you are planning a new product or redeveloping an existing one, ask your customers for their views on the existing product and what they would like to see in a new one. By explaining your plans and involving customers in product development, you can strengthen relationships and provide a service that is mutually beneficial. Questions could include:

◆ How can we improve the current product?

◆ What problems need to be overcome?

◆ What new features would customers welcome?

◆ Do the plans represent an improvement?

◆ Would customers make greater use of a product that includes the features they have highlighted?

> *Marketing secret*
>
> ◆ Involving customers at an early stage of product development is a key part of the research process.

Customer evaluation, or beta testing, is well established in the IT software industry. Customers test new products or upgraded versions before they are released to the market. They identify any problems in using the software, providing valuable feedback on product performance. Any problems or practical improvements can be incorporated before final release of the new product. Although there are important benefits to this type of collaboration, there are also risks. First, the customer may be extremely disappointed with the product if quality is poor. Second, there is a risk that competitors could find out about your plans indirectly. The quality issue is one that you should deal with: if a product is not right, it should not be given to customers in any form – it is not enough simply to promise future improvements. The security risk of a leak to competitors can be minimised through disclosure and confidentiality agreements, although these provide no real guarantee. However, the advantages of involving customers usually outweigh the risks, so evaluation is worthwhile in most cases.

Marketing secret

◆ Announcing your product plans helps customers formulate their own plans and smooths the way to a successful launch.

Another valuable practice from the IT industry is to pre-announce new products. For example, a company will set a number of release dates during the coming year when it will release new versions of products. The company outlines the new products and gives customers the opportunity to provide input to the development process. The major benefit for customers is that they can align their own business development plans to the release dates. They might, for example, postpone a particular project until the latest version of a product is released in six months' time. However, some companies have put themselves under unnecessary pressure by trying to meet a series of pre-announced release dates. The schedule may not allow proper time for development, resulting in failure to meet the date, or the release of a product that is not ready. Both are potentially damaging.

Set up joint development programmes

Product development can be a joint initiative where you work closely with specific customers to develop products that meet their specific needs. This approach is a valuable one in which:

◆ your customers have developed partnership sourcing to take advantage of your technology

◆ your customers have technology and technical skills that complement your own, and a joint project can produce more effective results

◆ you want to strengthen relationships with key customers by working in partnership on joint development projects.

There are different levels of collaboration. Some may involve regular meetings to provide input and review progress. These meetings can be held on site or remotely, using video-conference links. In some cases, customer staff may be seconded to work alongside the supplier team for all or part of the project. Secondments such as these can provide other benefits for the customer by improving the technical knowledge of their staff.

Marketing secret

◆ Involving customers in product development provides the detailed input on customer needs that may not be revealed through research alone.

Product development should be focused on customer needs. Although most companies carry out research before development, the research may not provide the detailed input that is essential. Product development may also be driven by technology, with no clear market focus. The more your customer depends on your product, the more likely it is to succeed, so involving customers can pay real dividends.

product development should be focused on customer needs

The new products you develop could enable your business customers to improve their competitive performance, so it is important to understand their markets. Tell business customers about your product plans and ask them for input to your development process. By building a detailed picture of their markets, you can align your own plans with theirs, and develop products that are tailored to their needs. There are some key questions to ask:

◆ What are their main markets?

◆ What is their position in the marketplace?

◆ Who are their main competitors?

◆ How are their products regarded in the marketplace?

◆ What are the key success factors in the market?

◆ What are the long-term product trends?

◆ What new technical developments will be needed to succeed?

◆ Could innovation by you help your customers to succeed?

◆ Are your customers considering entry into new markets?

◆ Do you have product development plans that are relevant to the new market?

It is equally important to understand your customers' business strategies: their corporate direction and key objectives, and how they aim to succeed. By aligning your product development objectives with theirs, and showing how your products or services can help them to achieve their strategic business objectives, you can ensure that your new products will be successful.

There are two important approaches to customer-focused product development:

1   Where your customers want to become market leaders through innovation, your new product programmes can help them develop the right level of innovation without investment in their own skills.

2   Where they want to succeed through competitive pricing, you can help them reduce overall costs by developing cost-effective products.

Marketing secret

◆ Products that help your customers to meet their strategic business objectives can increase the chances of new product success.

The more your customers depend on your new product, the more likely you are to succeed. For example, if your customer must develop new products quickly in order to retain and protect market share, your own new products can be critical to their product development programme. Other examples include instances in which your customers must reduce their cost base in order to compete effectively, and your new products can help them to succeed, or instances in which your products can play a vital role in improving their levels of customer satisfaction.

In assessing new product development opportunities, you should analyse how your products can help your customers. They can use your skills in a number of ways:

◆ Improving the performance of their own products and services by using your design and development skills. They may gain privileged access to your technical skills to improve their own competitive performance.

◆ Using your technical expertise to enhance the skills of their own technical staff, enabling them to make a more effective contribution to their own product development process.

◆ Using your technical resources to handle product development on a subcontract basis. This provides your partners with access to specialist resources or to additional research and development capacity to improve the performance of their product development programmes.

◆ Using your technical expertise to develop new products that they could not achieve themselves. This provides your customers with new technology, and allows them to diversify in line with your specialist skills.

◆ Using your design skills to improve through-life costs (the total cost of owning and using a product, including purchase price, maintenance, and any other related costs). By carrying out value engineering studies on your customers' products, you may be able to reduce overall costs and improve reliability by designing components that are easier to assemble and maintain.

Set up a user group

You can encourage feedback and build a sense of community by setting up a user group. The user group would operate as a forum for discussing issues of mutual concern to customers, such as quality, performance, standards, future developments, and customer concerns. The group would include representatives from your own company and from a cross-section of your customers. Comments from the user group provide valuable feedback on current perform-ance and help to identify needs that can be met through new product development. However, there are many examples of companies who have set up user groups in response to a crisis and then failed to use the information gathered. This can be frustrating for customers and wasteful for the companies. User groups provide a valuable perspective on products and service, and their feedback can provide real benefits for the product development process.

user groups provide a valuable perspective

Offer customers product configuration

Customers can make a direct contribution to the product development process by getting involved in the ways described above, but there is also an indirect form of involvement where customers choose their own product specification. When Dell first allowed customers to configure personal computers online, they revolutionised e-commerce. Buyers were no longer limited to standard, pre-packaged solutions. Now, customers can expect manufacturers to offer products configurable to their needs and to deliver them quickly.

Allowing customers to configure their own products gives them greater choice and enables you to gain a better understanding of customer preferences. The Dell model gives buyers a choice of standard features with a simplified selection process. Each selection is priced as an addition or subtraction from the base price option and may include free upgrades on certain features. The model also includes information on the benefits of choosing different features with comparisons between alternative choices. Customers can visit other parts of the website to read product reviews and customer feedback. They have the option to download brochures and can edit their choices at any stage before purchase. If they don't want to buy immediately, customers can create different versions and save them for comparison or later purchase.

Marketing secret
◆ Allowing customers to configure their own products gives them an indirect role in product development.

With configurable products, customers input their own preferences and a factory will custom-make them. Software systems provide you with the tools to assign any number of features to a configurable product, and organise them in meaningful categories that are shown to the user as menus or check boxes. As the customer selects different features, the price builds and changes so that they see the results of their choices immediately.

To help customers who are not sure of their requirements, you can suggest a default configuration or standard product that customers can choose 'as is' or edit as they wish. The default configuration and price should reflect good value for money and include the features that have proved most popular with other customers. The product's final price is instantly updated based on your default selections and the choices made by the user.

This is a proven commercially-successful model that can be applied to products and services that are available with options. Nonetheless, some commentators question the viability of the configurable business model given the cost issues and logistical problems arising from customised production and individual product fulfilment. They believe that it may not be suitable for products that return small profit margins per unit, particularly mass market products where price is the major deciding factor. Customisation is not suitable for products that have few options or for products that are low value.

Help customers make the right selection

Customers may need help in assessing the different features and options available. You can build in menus that provide detailed information on each feature as well as comparisons between different features. This can help to simplify the buying process, improve customer confidence and ensure a sale. You can go a step further and show a list of alternative products based on price range, performance application or other criteria. It is also possible to create feature comparison charts that summarise the functions that different models are best suited for.

Marketing secret

◆ Product configuration systems put customers in control of the buying process.

To encourage customers to complete their purchase, you can include special offers or free upgrades to higher specification on certain product features. This can make the final product more attractive or give price advantages over competitors. You can also make offers such as free delivery on products over a certain price point to influence customer selections.

Build-to-order systems may offer a number of display options that control the way configurable options are presented to the customer. For example, you can choose between radio buttons or drop-down menus, use alternating background colours for tables of specifications, and incorporate pop-up windows to provide the customer with more details about the options available for selection. For more complex sites, you can incorporate interactive 3D product visualisation that allows customers to rotate, tilt or magnify product images as they change configuration. This feature is useful when design or appearance is important and customers can select different finishes, colours or sizes. Once they have made their selections, customers should have the ability to save the product or service that they have configured to their account so that they can print it, edit it or submit it as an order at any time.

Make the system easy to use

If you plan to sell configurable products online the rule is the easier, the better. The first priority is to make information complete and easy to navigate. You can optimise the process by encouraging feedback from customers through emails, phone calls, site and phone metrics, focus groups, usability studies and online surveys. Responsiveness is key to the success of product configuration. The system should maximise the opportunity for interactivity while minimising the possibility of error. Key features should include:

make information complete and easy to navigate

◆ Flagging incompatible options and highlighting options that are compatible with the current choice.

◆ Providing appropriate help messages and up-selling and cross-selling suggestions.

◆ Providing graphics and animations to support product configuration.

◆ Simple pricing models.

There should also be a purchase assistance menu that includes payment options, information on tax and shipping, returns, privacy and online security, as well as account, product, shopping, order and technical support information, including the top frequently asked questions (FAQs). Contact information for sales enquiries or telephone ordering should be prominent.

Once the customer has configured their product, the system should generate order-ready quotes and likely delivery dates. This means that it is important to integrate your website functionality with back-office systems, the supply chain and finance partners so that the production and delivery process is smooth.

Build understanding and loyalty

Product customisation can deliver benefits of increased customer satisfaction by giving you the opportunity to get a better understanding of the wants and needs of your customers. Customisation can be one of the easiest ways to find out what customers really want and is a useful tool for generating customer feedback. Tapping into and delivering what customers want creates a powerful knowledge base that can be used to improve future product development.

Marketing secret

◆ Product customisation provides valuable insight into customer needs and preferences.

Some companies use product customisation as a built-in market research tool to source potential new brands that emerge as a result of overwhelming customer demand for particular configurations. This should lead to offers and products that more closely reflect customer needs. Because customers get a perfect match when they customise a product, this can increase loyalty even further.

As customers increasingly demand online self-service options, there are potential benefits to both parties. Greater customer convenience can also enable you to improve your own operational efficiency, as well as generating significant savings compared with the cost of processing sales and delivering support through call centres or field representatives.

Closer to your customers

One of the major marketing principles is understanding your customers' needs. Involving customers in designing and developing their own products is a good way to achieve that. It greatly reduces the risk of developing new products that might not hit the mark, because customers are involved from the outset. Involving your customers in product development and configuration also strengthens relationships through increased contact, and that can prove vital to your long-term success.

customers are involved from the outset

However, in many companies, customer contact takes place at a much more routine level. So, as far as those day-to-day contacts are concerned, are you confident that your company is doing all it can to satisfy your customers? The next chapter explains how to deal effectively with the many different forms of customer contact.

5

Pass the parcel – make it easier for customers to contact you

DO YOUR CUSTOMERS HAVE TO find their way through a maze of different phone numbers to get an answer? Do they get passed from extension to extension once they're through? More importantly, do the people answering the customer calls have access to all customer records, purchase history, emails, service requests and complaints? A single point of contact and an integrated customer record can make it easier to deal with every customer contact effectively.

Move the call centre on

When you contact a call centre, you know the scenario – the first call gets answered quickly and then you get put on hold. When someone answers, you find that they can't answer your query, so you get transferred to another person, sometimes unsuccessfully. And each time, you have to repeat all your details so that the agent can access your file ... again. It can be very frustrating. But there is a better way, and the technology available in the latest contact centre solutions is the key.

Contact centres can play a strategic role as the focal point of customer interactions, sales initiatives and profit generation. The quality of customer service in the contact centre can be a key differentiator in acquiring and retaining customers. That doesn't mean you have to operate a large call/contact centre. The same technology can be used by small numbers of customer-facing staff to provide a consistent quality service.

Marketing secret

◆ The quality of customer contact can be a key differentiator in acquiring and retaining customers.

This is important because customer expectations are rising. While technologies like interactive voice response, computer-telephony integration and call routing have significantly enhanced the customer experience, customers continually demand further improvement. They expect each interaction to be at least as satisfactory as the previous one, and this can put additional strains on your staff, who are probably already over-stretched. Today, customers expect to save time and money by using the web or email. They want responsive, personal service any time, anywhere, by any method they choose. Consumers and businesses are increasingly using interactive television, the Internet and mobile phones to obtain information and purchase a growing range of goods and services. Companies that rely on traditional call centres are therefore at a severe disadvantage.

Faced with the constant pressure to generate revenue, manage rising traffic volumes and meet ever-increasing customer service expectations, the traditional way of handling customer contact is no longer adequate. Customer demand and technological developments mean that you now have to offer the same standard of service over all communications channels – including voice, email, web and interactive communications.

the traditional way of handling customer contact is no longer adequate

---

Marketing secret

◆ Customers want to contact you by a method of their choice, not yours.

Customer choice is the real determining factor. But there is a paradox. Even if much of your business comes via the Internet, experience indicates that customers like to have the reassurance of live contact via the telephone for more complex inquiries. A contact strategy that covers all the main communication channels is now essential.

◆ Call centres have given customers a high standard of service for telephone contact. However, customers now expect the same standards of service from other communications channels. They want quick, convenient contact and a quality response every time they get in touch with a company, whichever channel they use.

◆ Companies that do not integrate their customer service across all channels may fail to acquire a complete profile of their customers, and so may be unable to deliver consistent standards of service. Integrating all channels in a contact centre provides a single view of all customer contacts and gives the opportunity to develop stronger customer relationships.

◆ Companies who rely on a traditional call centre cannot handle new communication channels effectively. Adding new facilities in an ad-hoc way leads to poor productivity and lack of integration.

Set the right contact strategy

Your customer contact strategy must balance cost, quality and revenue goals. The right contact strategy serves as the gateway to customer interactions that play an important role in generating revenue. It can also make an important contribution to profitability through a combination of cost savings and revenue generation:

◆ Utilising self-service options can minimise call levels, while freeing staff to focus on higher value customers.

◆ Identifying and supporting potential sales ensures that staff can optimise revenue opportunities through cross-selling and up-selling.

◆ Quality customer service levels can also improve profitability by increasing customer retention.

You can derive more benefit from your contact strategy by tying operational performance to key business objectives and priorities. For example, if you are aiming for revenue growth, you should focus your contact team on efforts to optimise sales. If you want to increase customer retention, you should set the operational levels of the contact centre to maximise customer satisfaction.

Marketing secret

◆ The best customer contact strategy derives the highest possible value from each contact.

A key objective is to derive the highest possible value from each call. That can take different forms, from simply meeting the customer's expectations, to closing a new sale, and requires a careful balance between cost, quality and revenue generation objectives. Generating a cross-sell also requires a significant time investment, which can increase costs and potentially affect service levels to other customers.

Get resources right

One of the greatest customer contact challenges is responding to fluctuating traffic. It's a familiar problem in contact centres, which can struggle to meet peaks in demand or utilise idle resources when traffic drops. These challenges arise due to unpredictable events: for example, calls to Internet Service Providers often spike sharply when there is a network problem. Similarly, a power failure or burst water main can quickly generate high call levels for a utility company. Unfortunately, contact centre staffing levels are generally decided well in advance, making it difficult to respond quickly to unexpected events. On the one hand, allocating contact centre staff conservatively can lead to poor service when traffic spikes. As queue times rise, customers become frustrated, and companies experience high levels of abandoned calls. On the other hand, over-scheduling the number of staff raises costs.

Another challenge is to match different contact centre tasks to individual staff capabilities. Some customer contact staff are expert at handling inbound calls, while others are equally comfortable handling inbound and outbound calls. Others may prefer to handle only non-voice channels such as email, web chat and instant messaging. Having staff focused on one interaction creates imbalances, particularly when there are peaks in traffic.

Marketing secret

◆ Customer-focused staff plus the right technology gives you a winning combination for effective customer contact.

This is a familiar problem whether you've got a small team handling telephone contact or a large contact centre, but this is where technology can help. Advanced call routing and call management capabilities mean that incoming calls can be handled in different ways. At peak hours, calls can be diverted to different members of the team, even if they are on different sites. Sophisticated systems allow calls to be diverted to the most appropriate person, with routing based on skills, product line, or the importance of the customer.

This can enhance the quality of customer service and increase customer satisfaction. Customer-focused routing is essential to maximise the potential from each call. Every interaction must be matched with the ideal person, regardless of location.

allow calls to be diverted to the most appropriate person

◆ To maximise sales potential, customer-focused routing connects callers with the highest skilled person.

◆ To maximise customer service outcomes, customers are routed to the person that helped them previously.

◆ To provide high levels of service to every customer during peak hours, customer-focused routing directs interactions to back-up resources.

Sometimes, meeting specific customer requirements takes specialised skills. It's therefore essential to provide access to the skills and resources of expert staff in other locations. For example, high-value banking clients can be immediately routed to a specialist in a branch office when conducting a complex transaction that may offer an up-sell opportunity.

To meet those fluctuating challenges, it's important to have a flexible contact team structure. At a basic level, staff could shift between activities according to their particular skill set and availability to handle different types of call or manage both inbound and outbound calls. Another approach is to reallocate staff from other areas of the company or other locations. These resources could be deployed at short notice to help manage high traffic volumes or handle complicated, specialised calls.

The key to success is to make the best use of your customer contact staff by predicting needs based on past traffic volumes. By combining good planning with the technology of customer-focused routing, you can get resource levels right by adjusting schedules and allocating staff to alternative tasks. This process can be improved even further by integrated training to ensure that contact staff skills evolve in line with changing demands.

The quality of call information is important too. Effective reporting systems do not simply highlight the source and timing of customer calls, they also draw attention to potential weaknesses in the ways incoming calls are handled. With the right management information, it becomes far easier to plan and monitor capacity, training and quality measures. It also allows the marketing team to measure the effectiveness of campaigns, and to fine-tune future programmes.

Integrate all communication channels

Many call centres are still based on voice contact alone, but customers have moved on. To be successful, you can no longer offer just great products and services; you must also meet and exceed customers' service expectations across all communication channels. A web-enabled contact strategy that can integrate all customer communications is now a top priority. Many customers prefer to interact with a company through non-voice channels such as email, text, chat or website. Integrating these channels ensures that customers receive a consistent customer experience across all means of contact. In the new model, traditional telephone contact mixes with the latest in online collaborative technology:

◆ Customers will have a choice, from simultaneous interactive voice and data access over the Internet, to the use of web pages as a self-service facility.

◆ For simple queries, staff can use instant text chat, email or web pages to handle questions or resolve problems quickly and easily.

◆ Customers who need to talk to a specialist can request a telephone call back automatically from a web page.

While none of these types of communication is new, linking them together in a single unified interface is revolutionary. Integrating all these channels provides the customer with the same experience, no matter how they choose to communicate with the company.

Enhance service and sales

Collaboration and response provide a superb foundation for delivering the highest standards of customer service. The other major benefit of integration is the vast amount of data available from the customer channels.

Marketing secret

◆ Every form of contact yields valuable customer data. Use that to enhance the quality of service even further.

That information can be used to reduce the customer decision-making interval and close the sale cycle effectively and efficiently. It also increases cross-selling and up-selling opportunities, and supports customer-focused marketing strategies. Customers who contact you should enjoy a consistent high-quality experience on every occasion:

◆ Efficient management of queue and handling times ensures that customer frustration is managed without putting pressure on staff to rush calls.

◆ Customers can use any preferred interaction channel to communicate with you, including self-service, with a consistent experience and positive result.

◆ By recognising a customer's value and requirements, you should be able to match the customer with the ideal member of staff.

◆ Proactive contact should give customers 'peace of mind' by providing them with relevant and timely information.

Proactive contact can take the form of an outbound call, email or text to promote a product, provide important information, or keep customers up to date. For example, this approach can help avert unplanned call peaks by proactively calling customers after a power cut, cancelled flight or other event that is likely to trigger high levels of inbound calls.

To increase customer satisfaction rates and revenue, it's important to anticipate customer needs when they are open to purchasing. Giving staff customised information that tailors product and service recommendations to the customer's profile, purchase history and type of call can help to improve results. This, as the next section explains, is at the heart of the 360-degree view of the customer.

Get a 360-degree view of your customers

Customers can interact with many different departments or contacts in your company. To build the most effective and profitable relationship with a customer, it's essential for everyone in a company to have access to the full 360-degree view of customer transactions. Putting all customer details, purchases, contacts, enquiries and service records on an intranet can provide the essential information your sales and marketing teams need.

The 360-degree view tells you how your customers are contacting you, browsing your website, acquiring information, ordering products, placing service enquiries or making complaints.

Marketing secret

◆ The 360-degree view brings together all customer information to build a detailed profile and demonstrate how well your sales, marketing and communication channels match your customers' activities.

Technology plays an important role because companies who want the 360-degree view must have a suitable networking solution that integrates all the customer information that is available in separate parts of an organisation. However, it is also an approach to business which puts the customer at the centre of the organisation and builds a platform for quality customer service.

Most companies have detailed customer records, but how many are aware of all the customer interactions that take place? Very few have a 360-degree view of the customer – that is, a single view of all customer interactions. Getting a 360-degree view is essential if you want to optimise marketing, communications, customer service and product development. Used effectively, the 360-degree view strengthens customer retention and can increase customers' lifetime value and profitability. Looking ahead, when you've got a 360-degree view, you can tailor products and services to meet customers' long-term needs, confident that you have a complete picture of their needs, challenges and purchase history.

the 360-degree view strengthens customer retention

The 360-degree approach underpins a number of important customer service initiatives:

◆ Development of measurable goals, objectives and tactics for every point of interaction customers have with your company.

◆ Establishment of company-wide business metrics, customer measurement, tracking and reporting processes for all sectors, product lines and points of contact.

◆ Development of customer interaction guidelines for every part of your company that has customer contact.

Make customer-facing staff more effective

Customer information is often scattered across several business systems, making it difficult for customer service representatives to gain a 360-degree view of the customer when they are making contact. As a result, staff waste valuable time navigating several applications to piece together a single view of the customer. They may also miss opportunities to make inbound customer enquiries more productive because they lack intelligence about the customer, such as the customer's disposition to buy certain products.

Networked computer solutions provide an efficient and effective method of creating a single view of the customer or a single view of a process. The system integrates your other business systems for customer-facing staff, providing them with a comprehensive view of the customer that can be used to simplify access to customer information and dramatically improve productivity, morale, and – most importantly – your customers' experience.

A 360-degree solution enables you to consolidate customer data such as transaction history, payment history, or other information from separate applications, and deliver a simple view that each member of staff can use to provide the information a customer is requesting without having to navigate a maze of screens. Your customers want information and services – fast. Providing your staff with a single view of the customer can have a significant impact on their ability to deliver superior *your customers want* customer service. By reducing the amount *information and* of time and frustration it takes to switch *services – fast* between multiple applications to handle calls, you're giving staff greater flexibility, enabling them to spend less time interacting with systems and more time interacting with customers. Having full knowledge at their fingertips means that staff can close each enquiry successfully, without having to refer to other people or other systems.

Marketing secret

◆ Providing your staff with a single view of the customer can have a significant impact on their ability to deliver superior customer service.

The ability to deliver a high-quality customer experience using a 360-degree view of the customer can be of major strategic value to your company. Having a single view of the customer right at your staff's fingertips means that you have a greater opportunity to cultivate a more meaningful relationship with that customer, either by solving a problem or offering additional products or services that generate additional revenue. The 360-degree view enables your staff to increase customer satisfaction by engaging in knowledgeable conversations with the customer, confident that they have full up-to-date information available when they need it.

Offer customers a consistent experience

The 360-degree view doesn't just offer a consolidated view of the customer, it also provides staff with access to information needed to meet customer-service demands and support web-based customer self-service. The system can also guide staff through processes such as cross-selling interactions, which allows you to introduce best practices into every customer interaction. The result is that customers will enjoy a consistent experience throughout your company. This level of consistency also provides important productivity benefits for your sales and customer service operations:

♦ Improved customer interaction and call quality.

♦ Reduced call time.

♦ Significant reduction in data entry errors.

♦ Reduced training time.

Customer service and sales operations based on a 360-degree view give you the opportunity to provide your customers with a one-stop shop – a single point of contact for all your products and services. This can be particularly useful if your company has a number of product lines sold through different departments or divisions. Customers don't want to spend their time being transferred between departments or trying to work out for themselves who they should contact. Ideally, any member of your customer-facing team should be able to deal with any type of customer enquiry. It may be that certain enquiries have to be escalated or transferred to specialists, but this can be handled seamlessly, without inconveniencing the customer.

Increasingly, customers are making buying decisions based on more than the four traditional factors of product, place, price and promotion. They are also influenced by variables such as service quality, recognition and efficiency of customer support. With a 360-degree system in place, you may be able to strongly differentiate your company in these areas and achieve high levels of customer satisfaction.

> ### Marketing secret
>
> ◆ Relationships with customers are not possible without understanding who your customers really are, what they value, what they want to buy, and how they prefer to interact with and be served by you.

The 360-degree view is an integral element of customer relationship management. Relationships with customers are not possible without understanding who your customers really are, what they value, what they want to buy, and how they prefer to interact with and be served by you. Moving your customer relationships forward requires a deeper understanding of customer characteristics and behaviours, such as your customers' purchases and related spending patterns, their current potential value to your company, and other characteristics.

Creating a single point of contact for all customer enquiries is an important strategic objective, but to achieve it, you may have to overcome internal resistance. The 360-degree approach replaces separate functions such as call centres, help desks, customer service departments and sales offices, as well as individual account managers. People in these areas may feel that they have a strong relationship with certain customers and may be unwilling to give up 'ownership'. You need to demonstrate the benefits of the 360-degree approach to all customer-facing staff and win their commitment to the new approach.

win their commitment to the new approach

The 360-degree approach is based on networking technologies that integrate information from separate departments and IT systems. However, it is the people who interact with customers who deliver the real benefits. They must be committed to the single point of contact approach and they must be able to use the full facilities of the system so that they are able to deliver prompt, quality service and recognise opportunities to win new business.

Make it a great experience

So, you've made the investment in marketing, raised the customer's interest and encouraged them to contact your company. But what happens when the customer makes contact? The first experience can make or break a relationship and that's why customer contact is so important. Get it right and you're on the way to a great relationship that keeps the customer coming back. No wonder so many companies put 'improving the customer experience' as one of their top priorities.

This opening section has emphasised the importance of quality contact as a means of strengthening customer relationships. It demonstrates that success is not just dependent on great products. The next section of the book takes that further and looks at other factors that impact on marketing success.

PART 2

It takes more than a product to succeed

Great products are critical to the marketing effort, but they will succeed only if customers understand the product benefits and the factors that differentiate you from your competitors. This section explains the role that branding plays and shows how services can add real value to your product offering. Thought leadership can strengthen your brand even further and help to build an understanding and sense of value that overcomes any price issues.

6 Piggyback on other brands

Some companies have no obvious identity of their own in the eyes of consumers. That's a real problem for component manufacturers in particular. But why keep quiet? Intel, the chip manufacturer, supplies just one small component to computer manufacturers. But 'Intel Inside' is often more recognisable than the brand name of the computer itself.

7 Service charge is extra

One capital goods company used to include services like installation, maintenance and support as part of the overall purchase price as part of an incentive to buy – a decision that was popular with the salesforce. When research indicated that their customers found these services valuable and would be willing to pay for them, sometimes from third-party suppliers, the company set up a service division, developed a portfolio of chargeable services and launched them. Within a year, that division became the most profitable in the company and the salesforce suffered no loss of business.

8 Sell the knowledge

An important part of brand building is thought leadership, demonstrating the quality and breadth of your company's knowledge of the marketplace – how well you understand your customers' needs and the challenges they face. You can build a position of thought leadership by publishing white papers, participating in industry seminars and contributing to customer industry magazines.

9 Risky business – pricing in challenging times

How do you set prices in challenging economic conditions? Competing on price alone to maintain market share may be risky. It's therefore important to retain a balance and continue concentrating on performance and quality factors that differentiate your business. By identifying the pricing factors that are important to customers, you can use that knowledge to win and retain business.

6

Piggyback on other brands

SOME COMPANIES HAVE NO obvious identity of their own in the eyes of consumers. That's a real problem for component manufacturers in particular. As an example, Intel, the microprocessor manufacturer, supplies just one small component to computer manufacturers. But the phrase 'Intel Inside' is often more recognisable than the brand name of the computer itself. It's not just component manufacturers who can 'piggyback' on other brands. If you have strong established brands, you can use their strength to extend your range and benefit from the same brand values. The Intel story shows just how effective this process can be.

Strong branding makes a difference

In most products, the components go almost unnoticed. Branding a component is typically seen as a waste of money because the feeling is that most customers don't care what's inside a product as long as it works well. Intel changed all that by building a powerful brand that has helped to make it the largest chip manufacturer in the world.

The company recognised the need for branding when it found that competitors were adopting the same naming conventions on products that Intel had pioneered and it was unable to protect trade names like '286', '386' and '486'. Intel was looking for a way to create a clear identity in a confusing commodity marketplace. The 'Intel Inside' programme took the form of cooperative advertising with leading computer manufacturers with the objective of creating a premium brand for both partners.

Marketing secret

◆ Strong branding is essential to create a clear identity in a confusing commodity marketplace.

Intel convinced manufacturers that their computers would have higher perceived value if they featured Intel in their own marketing by using the 'Intel Inside' logo in their advertising and other marketing material. The campaign aimed to educate both retailers and consumers about the value of Intel chips, and to explain to them the differences between the different types of microprocessors. The campaign took away the mystery of the product, convincing consumers that 'Intel Inside' represented quality and reliability.

educate both retailers and consumers

At the outset of the campaign, the company's own research indicated that only 24 per cent of European personal computer buyers were familiar with the 'Intel Inside' logo. A year later, the figure was almost 80 per cent and, within four years, it had reached 94 per cent. Through this branding programme, Intel raised awareness for microprocessors in general and for its own brand. Decision makers now paid close attention to the computer components before making a purchase and Intel was perceived as the standard for quality. And because Intel is linked with premium computer brands, it created the impression that Intel itself is a premium brand.

Marketing secret

◆ A strong brand image can convince customers that it is worth paying a premium for a superior product.

Market research has indicated that end-users show a strong preference for computer systems containing Intel microprocessors. Around 70 per cent of home computer buyers and 85 per cent of business buyers state a preference for Intel, saying they will pay a premium for the security and peace-of-mind offered by the brand.

The success of the 'Intel Inside' campaign can be attributed to a number of factors, including:

◆ an established reputation for producing leading-edge technology, in particular microprocessors

◆ a willingness to proactively collaborate with channel partners

◆ the adoption of industry leading marketing strategies, such as the use of plain English packaging and component instructions

◆ an aggressive marketing budget, which maintained substantial campaign spend.

One of Intel's main competitors, AMD, responded indirectly to Intel's dominance by positioning itself as a brand that makes the microprocessor decision easier for the customer. Since there is no clear formula for relating functions such as burning a DVD or carrying out multiple tasks to the technical specification of a microprocessor, customers have to put their trust in the salesperson's product knowledge or in a so-called independent review. With the increasing performance of most personal computers, customers can be left feeling even more confused. The AMD branding aims to relate the chip model to the customer requirement. The customer should be able to go to a retailer and say: 'Here's what I want to do with my computer, what chip should I use?' The AMD range was divided into six products, each with clear functional capability related to customer's actual use.

The added bonus for customers is that AMD's policy is to introduce the highest levels of functionality on its premium brands and then filter that functionality down through the range, eventually right down to the base model. At the same time, the company would augment the performance of its higher level products so that customers could see a policy of continuous enhancement.

Extend successful brands

It is important to be proactive in managing and extending your brands to retain competitive advantage. Brands can be extended in many different ways, from enhancing a product with additional features and benefits, to varying the product for different market sectors. Existing products can go through a continuous process of review and development to ensure that they remain focused on changing customer needs. There are a number of different approaches to brand extension, including:

be proactive in managing and extending your brands

- enhancing the product with additional features and benefits
- introducing higher- or lower-priced versions
- increasing the range
- using product variants to segment the market
- introducing niche products
- introducing own label products
- buying in products or services from third parties
- responding to competitive product actions.

Enhance the product

Enhancing the product with additional features and benefits is a suitable strategy for developing existing products in a growth or mature phase. The enhancements can be based on an assessment of customer needs or a policy of matching competitive actions. It can take a number of forms:

- improving performance or enhancing the product to provide a competitive edge
- improving performance to reflect customer requirements
- enhancing the product while maintaining the same price.

Product developments like this can be easily imitated, so they may provide only short-term competitive advantage. However, they focus on customer requirements and demonstrate that the brand's emphasis is on leading rather than following.

Introduce higher- or lower-priced versions

Price may be an inhibiting factor for prospective customers. Introducing a lower-priced version may broaden the market for the brand. However, in producing the budget version, you should ensure that you do not dilute any of the brand values that differentiate the product. If quality, for example, is a key brand value, there should be no reduction in quality standards. Customer perception of the whole range could be affected by reports of poor quality.

do not dilute any of the brand values

Higher-priced versions can increase revenue. By offering existing customers a higher-priced version, you can build on customer satisfaction with existing brand values. You should ensure that the higher-priced version continues to offer value for money. Simply raising the price of an existing product could alienate existing customers.

Increase the range

Increasing the range allows you to build on the reputation and success of your existing brand to sell more products through the same sales channels. The strategy has a number of important benefits:

◆ Products added to an existing range offer customers a greater choice.

◆ The additional products may make the range more attractive to prospective customers.

◆ The new products benefit from the marketing support given to existing products in the range.

◆ A range strategy provides an opportunity to increase the value of sales per customer, without a proportional increase in marketing costs.

◆ Range extension is an important element of a relationship marketing programme.

This approach reduces the overall cost and risk of new product development. It builds on the strength of existing brands and is therefore difficult for your competitors to imitate. It is focused on customer needs and utilises customer relationships to improve sales channel performance. The difficult decision is whether to extend the range with similar products or to introduce entirely new types of product. Introducing similar products makes it more likely that customers will accept the new offers due to the familiarity factor. Introducing new types of product carries a higher risk.

Use product variants to segment the market

This strategy is based on the refinement of existing products to meet the requirements of different market sectors. By adopting this strategy, you can concentrate on meeting the precise needs of individual sectors and focus resources on the most important ones. You will also enhance the brand's perception and build stronger relationships with customers in individual sectors. The approach also builds on the strength of existing products, and is therefore difficult for your competitors to imitate.

Introduce niche products

You can concentrate on the whole market or on specific niche sectors where you have strengths or opportunities that are not available to competitors. This approach delivers low volumes but usually higher prices. It shows that the brand meets specific customer requirements, but success will depend on highly-targeted marketing. The low potential return can discourage certain types of competitor, but it also allows smaller companies to compete effectively with larger organisations.

Introduce own label products

If you market products under your own brand name, you can also increase sales by developing modified products for sale by other organisations under their name. The strategy has a number of possible approaches:

◆ Repackaging standard products in the own label identity.

◆ Modifying the product to meet the other manufacturer's specifications.

◆ Developing a product specifically for the other manufacturer.

Own label development reduces the cost of product development while generating income. It uses brand strengths to increase sales to third parties but reduces the opportunity for you to improve market share for your own products.

Buy in products or services from third parties

This strategy, like the own label strategy, allows you to increase your own range and extend your brand without investing in your own product development. There are a number of possible approaches:

◆ Subcontract product development to an outside organisation.

◆ Buy existing products that complement or extend a range.

◆ Buy a complete product range from a third party.

◆ Work in partnership with a third party jointly to develop a new product or service.

Buying in products reduces the cost of your own product development and ensures a fast time-to-market. However, the same products could also be sourced by your competitors and there is no guarantee that the bought-in products will offer the same level of quality and performance as your own products. Any reduction of standards could have an adverse effect on brand perceptions.

Respond to competitive actions

This strategy is important if you are in a competitive marketplace. By matching competitive actions, you can ensure that you retain market share. This type of strategy would include the following actions:

◆ Matching your products to those of your competitors.

◆ Aiming at small improvements in performance to maintain competitive advantage.

◆ Monitoring market developments, rather than pursuing a programme of innovation.

◆ Utilising high levels of marketing support to compensate for low product differentials.

◆ Using loyalty programmes to retain customers.

The strategy reduces the cost and risk of new product development, but it focuses on retaining market share rather than market development. The product developments can be easily imitated, so there is minimal competitive advantage. The strategy could result in a defensive attitude that does not take your company forward: it puts the emphasis on following rather than leading. It can also be difficult to catch up if a competitor introduces a major change.

Update successful brands

Some companies rely on the success of their existing products and introduce products in a haphazard way, hoping that customers will buy the new product just because it carries an established brand name. However, customers will judge a product on its performance and its ability to meet their needs, not just on its brand name.

Nonetheless, it is easy to overlook the extension opportunities offered by a strong brand. Developing or introducing new products that promise customers the same brand values can generate additional income and broaden the customer base.

Sometimes, if you've got a successful brand, you may be reluctant to change it. However, if customers need change or if

> ### Marketing secret
>
> ◆ Customers judge a product on its performance and its ability to meet their needs, not on its brand name. Don't try to cut corners when you extend a brand.

competitive products improve, the successful brand may begin to lose market share and may not recover. It's worth considering a brand extension if market conditions are favourable, as long as the new launch does not distract from your core brand activities. Introducing similar products can increase the likelihood of customer acceptance. However, the risk of bringing out a new product is that it could take sales from existing products in the range and may confuse customers.

If an existing brand is not performing well in the market or has quality problems, a new brand is unlikely to be well received. Furthermore, trying to extend a brand without maintaining product quality and without giving the new products adequate sales or marketing resources is extremely risky. Poor performance or product failures can damage the other products in the range, so extension must be carefully planned. A new product that draws on the strengths of the main brand may succeed without individual support. However, if the extension represents a change of direction for the brand, heavy marketing support will be important.

Keep customers informed of changes

When you are planning brand extensions, it pays to give customers an indication of your future direction. This is

give customers an indication of your future direction

particularly important when new products represent an upgrade from existing goods or when they form a platform for a new generation of products. A product roadmap can help customers understand how brand extension will affect them and how new products relate to your existing range.

Marketing secret

◆ Technology companies know that the way to keep customers and build long-term revenue is to keep announcing product upgrades. How does that work for your product range?

The roadmaps can take a number of different forms:

◆ **Product roadmap** – describes the timing and features of new products that you plan to release.

◆ **Market roadmap** – indicates the market sectors you will target with new offerings and describes the relevant products.

◆ **Vision** – indicates where your company would like to be in the market. For example, you could state your aim to be a market leader, or you could show how your brand developments fit into your company's vision of the market in the future.

◆ **Technology roadmap** – describes how your company's technology will evolve or how your products will take advantage of emerging technologies.

◆ **Product platform** – describes a set of standards for your next generation of products, allowing other companies to develop products that work with yours.

Build on the brand

A clear strong brand is the foundation for great marketing. You might be selling the most advanced product on the market, but, if your brand isn't recognised, you've got an uphill battle to build share. The way that component manufacturers like Intel created a new way of looking at their products shows how important branding can be, even in a commodity market. A strong brand will give your new products an extra push when they're launched, making your marketing budget work even harder.

And it's not just product branding that counts. For many companies, branding services plays an equally important role in building customer satisfaction, as the next chapter shows.

7

Service charge is extra

ONE CAPITAL GOODS COMPANY used to include services like installation, maintenance and support as part of the overall purchase price as part of an incentive to buy – a decision that was popular with the salesforce. When research indicated that their customers found these services valuable and would be willing to pay for them, sometimes from third-party suppliers, the company set up a service division, developed a portfolio of chargeable services and launched them. Within a year, that division became the most profitable in the company and the salesforce suffered no loss of business.

Extend a product with service

The above example demonstrates the value of customer services. Service is frequently relegated to maintenance and problem solving. However, it can be a key differentiator between you and the competition. Meeting customer requirements in the most appropriate and

it can be a key differentiator between you and the competition

efficient way adds enormously to the perceived value of your product.

Services can add further value to a product, providing incremental income and increasing customer loyalty. Services provide you with an opportunity to continue dealing with a customer long after the initial sale. Many companies have internal service departments; however, they can be expensive to maintain, and are sometimes lacking in essential skills. By demonstrating the potential savings and benefits of outsourcing service, you may be able to persuade your company to switch to an external source.

Marketing secret

◆ Services provide you with an opportunity to continue
   dealing with a customer long after the initial sale.

Many companies have recognised the importance of service to their customers, and have changed their service strategy accordingly. Instead of offering free service, they have upgraded the services, widened their portfolio, and started charging customers for services. Although customers may initially object to being charged for something that was free, charging demonstrates the value of the service. To take full advantage of the service opportunity, it is important to explain the benefits of effective service to customers, and present your service operations as convenient, cost-effective, and strategically important.

*charging
demonstrates the
value of the service*

Add value to a product

Adding value to a product or service helps to differentiate products from the competition, and improves standards of customer service. By analysing the products and services in your range, you can add value and improve customers' perception of your organisation. Some examples are:

◆ Business services that free up customer staff to do more important tasks, or help managers perform their jobs better. For example, training can ensure that staff make more effective use of the products that the company buys.

◆ Accessories to make a consumer product, such as a camera, more attractive.

◆ Convenience services added to a basic service to enhance it. For example, insurance companies might add a helpline or list of approved repairers to help their customers recover more quickly from an accident.

Recognise service opportunities

Customers require many different services during the time they own a product – the ownership cycle. Their requirements could include advice, consultancy and design before the sale; installation and training; followed by maintenance, upgrading and other after-sales services. Each of these represents an opportunity to earn incremental income and maintain contact with the customer.

> *Marketing secret*
> ◆ Customers require many different services during the
>   time they own a product. Each service represents an
>   opportunity to earn incremental income and maintain
>   contact with the customer.

Outsourcing is a growing trend in companies seeking to
concentrate on their core business, rather than attempting
to do everything themselves. By using outside specialists to
handle activities such as maintenance, systems management,
distribution, fleet management and customer support, your
customers can make better use of their own resources and
benefit from a quality, cost-effective service from suppliers
who specialise in the activity. Outsourcing provides you with
an opportunity to build closer relations with your customers
by offering them vital services.

One of the most effective ways to identify service opportunities is to look at the problems your customers face by
analysing a series of business scenarios. Some examples
show how the process works:

◆ **Objective advice** – Your customers need to ensure
  that they have devised the right strategy to meet their
  business objectives. They need objective advice and
  guidance to improve the quality of their own decision
  making. You could meet those requirements by offering
  consultancy services.

◆ **Defining problems** – Your customers have identified
  certain activities which are crucial to their business

success. They need help in defining the problems and planning the most appropriate course of action. Consultancy will also be relevant here.

◆ **Adapt quickly to change** – Your customers need to adapt quickly to changing market conditions or competitive threats, but they do not have the resources or skills to succeed. You can offer your customers your skills and resources on a project basis so that they can meet both their short- and long-term requirements.

◆ **Develop new skills** – Your customers need to develop new user and management skills so that they can get the best return from the products and services they have bought from you. You can offer your customers training services.

◆ **Continued service operation** – Your customers need to ensure that their products are continually operational and providing the business benefits they were designed for. By offering your customers maintenance services or managing their equipment for them, you can ensure that their products are kept in the best possible condition.

These business scenarios help you to identify opportunities for offering services to your customers. Customers may provide many of these services from their own resources, but it is possible to get further involved through the growth in outsourcing.

Meet key service attributes

The table below shows some of the key features that customers are looking for in a service offer.

TABLE 7.1 *Key features of a service offer*

Service	Customer benefit
One contact point	Simplifies contact and service administration.
Nationwide resources	Support available wherever the customer is located.
Direct contact with a technical specialist	Immediate response to problems or queries.
Quality support to recognised standards	Independent reassurance that service standards are high.
Complete support solutions	Support to meet all customers' needs with consistent service standards.
Service options	Choice of service levels which can be aligned to customers' needs.
Investment in support	Long-term commitment to the customer.

Provide one contact point for service resources

Whether your customers have a technical query, a service request or a product enquiry, or need advice, guidance, or information, they should be able to call one number for direct access to all your support resources. Ideally, you'll have specialists on the spot to deal with all requests. If they can't answer the query straight away, make sure that the right person calls the customer back.

Offer direct contact with technical specialists

Your customers may have a technical query, and want to talk to an experienced specialist straight away. When they call the technical help desk, they should be talking to a highly-skilled person with extensive technical support and field experience.

Provide quality support

Superior service standards can differentiate a supplier, so it is important that you position your company as a quality service supplier. Your customers will assess your performance according to a number of factors:

position your company as a quality service supplier

◆ Adherence to an independent quality standard.

◆ Your service response mechanism – how quickly and easily customers can contact you when they have a query or a problem.

◆ Your service infrastructure – spares level, service network, location and number of service specialists, investment in service tools.

◆ Your service performance – response times, success rate, your measurement of customer satisfaction and your escalation procedures for problems that cannot be immediately resolved.

Develop complete support solutions

You should be able to provide complete support throughout the time your customers own the product. Develop a comprehensive service portfolio, including:

◆ consultancy

◆ application development

◆ finance

◆ installation

◆ systems integration

◆ training

◆ planned maintenance

◆ technical support.

Offer flexible service options

Provide your customers with a choice of flexible service options to suit their operational needs. If your customers have an in-house support operation, support their team with an efficient spares delivery service, or manage their spares for them. Also offer to enhance the skills of your customer's in-house team with training, advice and guidance, technical support, and access to specialists.

Invest in support

To meet key service attributes and deliver quality service requires a significant investment in the service infrastructure. The right service team, efficient service communications and a sophisticated service management system enable you to enhance your response and performance even further. Customers expect a quality service. If you fail to deliver the right standard of service, you could damage customer relationships. That means you have to

invest in people and infrastructure. You
can either build your own service team
with recruitment and training, or work in
partnership with a specialist organisation
which will deliver service on your behalf.

*invest in people and
infrastructure*

> *Marketing secret*
> ◆ Customers expect a quality service. If you fail to
>   deliver the right standard of service, you could damage
>   customer relationships.

Develop product/service packages

Basic services such as installation, maintenance and
upgrades are available from many different service organisations. They do not differentiate you and they do not add
value. Higher-value services, requiring skill, knowledge or
experience, are the keys to success. To add value to products
and to increase customer loyalty, put together 'bundles' of
products and services that reflect customer needs. The list
below shows examples of this.

All-inclusive services

◆ Package holidays, including flights, hotel, and transport.

◆ Out-of-town retail sites, with greater convenience of
  parking and distribution.

'No frills' services

◆ 'Fast-fit' car repair centres, offering essential services only.

◆ Direct banking without premises.

◆ Direct insurance without intermediaries.

Changing infrastructure services

◆ Electronic newspapers.

◆ Online shopping.

Added value services

◆ Home delivery of fast food.

◆ Personal breakdown/recovery/onward transport.

◆ Support and advice through helplines.

Changing distribution channels

◆ Direct sales, bypassing retailers.

◆ Electronic delivery, such as software downloads.

Use services to maintain account control

Look at your customers' buying cycle. How frequently do they make purchases – monthly, annually, every three years, every five years? The longer the purchase cycle, the more difficult it is to retain account control. Other companies can be talking to your customers, users may be experiencing problems that you are not aware of, and the decision-making team may be changing in ways that you cannot influence. Loss of contact could mean loss of control. In that situation, services can play a key role in maintaining contact and retaining account control.

> *Marketing secret*
>
> ◆ Services can play a key role in retaining account control.

In the consumer sector, car manufacturers realised that the period between new car sales is the most critical element of customer relations. With customers buying new cars every two to three years on average, sales control is minimal. Manufacturers have therefore focused their efforts on building an effective after-sales operation based on the fact that parts and service operations generate five times the number of customer contacts as new car sales. The manufacturers realised that they had been losing both repair and scheduled maintenance work to 'fast-fit' operations. This meant a loss of revenue to their dealerships, but also denied them the opportunity to maintain customer satisfaction between car purchases.

The same principle can be applied to markets where new product sales have similar purchase lead times of several years. Computer manufacturers had been losing maintenance business to independent service companies; they also found that the customers' information systems strategy and choice of systems was being driven, not by the manufacturers, but by management consultancies. When management

consultancies moved into other areas of information systems service, such as application development and managed
service, and, when independent service companies expanded
their activities, the computer manufacturers lost even more
account control. Although service companies and management consultancies were not the manufacturers' direct
competitors, they were enjoying high levels of contact with
key decision makers at senior and middle management
level, and this influenced future business opportunities. By
introducing a broad range of services themselves, the manufacturers would be able to build high levels of contact with
decision makers throughout the customer organisation.

Customer contact is one of the most important benefits
of a service programme. Here's what happened when a computer manufacturer decided to widen its service portfolio.
It was able to identify a number of stages where customer
service can be used to increase the frequency and quality of
customer contact.

- **Pre-sales consultancy** – Helping the customer develop a
  strategy in line with corporate objectives. This brings the
  company into contact with the senior executive team and
  provides valuable information on the customer's future
  business plans.

- **Planning services** – Turning the strategy into a practical
  solution. This provides contact opportunities at senior
  executive and operational levels.

- **Implementation services** – Helping the customer to
  install and introduce a new product without recruiting
  specialist staff or overloading their own support staff.

This helps to ensure that the customer's product is implemented effectively, increasing customer satisfaction and loyalty.

◆ **Training services** – Providing the customer with skills development and building useful contact with departmental managers and users.

◆ **Managed services** – These cover a wide range of maintenance services. These provide the supplier with one of the best opportunities for continuous contact with the customer and give the supplier a valuable insight into the customer's changing product needs.

Offer customers finance

Offering customers finance can often help to clinch a deal, particularly for a major capital purchase. However, simply offering basic finance may not be enough. By working in partnership with a specialist finance company you can offer customers a range of finance options tailored to their individual budget.

For many customers, the decision about how to purchase products is as critical as the decision about what is required. An effective funding decision must take into account a range of business, financial and technical considerations. That way, purchasing can be treated not as a cost, but as an opportunity to add value to the business.

Constant technological developments mean that your customers could find their existing equipment becoming obsolete. If they have leased the equipment from you, rather than purchasing outright, you can offer financing arrangements that allow customers to benefit from product upgrade options during the term of the agreement, without further capital investment. Expansion and market conditions could also change your customers' short- to medium-term investment needs. Financing allows them the option to upgrade or add further equipment within the terms of the original agreement.

Marketing secret

◆ Financing is becoming an increasingly important part of companies' total offer as customers recognise that financing purchases can bring forward business benefits, while preserving capital to grow other areas of their business.

Financing is becoming an increasingly important part of companies' total offer as customers recognise that financing purchases can bring forward business benefits, while preserving capital to grow other areas of their business. Financing provides essential equipment for predictable payment over an agreed term, protecting capital and improving cashflow. That means equipment can be put to productive use immediately, reducing costs, improving competitive performance, increasing efficiency and delivering other business benefits that can have a direct impact on the bottom line. That makes it extremely attractive to customers, as these two examples show.

When a leading UK building society merged with another financial institution, it recognised the barriers to business growth of its ageing telephone network. However, budgetary issues threatened to delay the project by 18 months, with significant impact on revenue and profitability for the merged operation. A finance solution that incorporated a deferred payment arrangement allowed the company to bring forward the project and pay for it in phases while the new network delivered immediate business benefit.

An international stock exchange wanted to enhance its competitive position by improving the availability of real-time market and trading data to customers. It also recognised that it would need to refresh its technology on a regular basis to maintain an edge over competitors. A financing deal was structured that enabled the exchange to refresh technology on an ongoing basis while minimising risk and exposure by providing the option to return equipment at the end of the term.

The true cost of equipment purchase goes beyond the cost of the hardware. It includes the cost of installation, training, maintenance and financing – the total cost of operations (TCO). A finance agreement can be structured to include all of the elements that contribute to TCO in a single predictable payment, enabling your customers to implement a complete solution, with the opportunity to lower TCO.

Marketing secret

◆ Financing is not just an alternative method of funding purchasing. It provides a strategic platform for delivering business, technical and financial benefits to your customers.

If you decide to offer your customers finance, it's important to choose the right finance partner. The supplier should have a good working knowledge of your market sector and the potential benefits of the products you offer so that it can tailor financial advice in a relevant way.

Services build relationships

Services can help to strengthen relationships with your customers, as well as providing incremental income and adding value to your products. Quality services also enhance your brand values. For many companies it can make or break their reputation, as one automotive manufacturer found out. 'Great cars, shame about the dealership service' was a common complaint until the company put a major investment into improving customer service at local level.

good service matters

In many sectors, smart customers recognise the value that good service can make to their own business. They've invested in your products and they want to get the best possible return from those products. Help them to use those products efficiently, keep them operating reliably and reduce the customer's whole life costs. That's why good service matters and why it's the foundation for great customer relationships.

An important element of that service offer is the quality of knowledge and expertise your customers can access. As the next chapter shows, demonstrating your knowledge can help you build a position of leadership in your market.

8

Sell the knowledge

AN IMPORTANT PART OF BRAND BUILDING is thought leadership, demonstrating the quality and breadth of your company's knowledge of the marketplace – how well you understand your customers' needs and the challenges they face. You can build a position of thought leadership by publishing white papers, participating in industry seminars and contributing to customer industry magazines. Thought leadership can be considered as part of a relationship marketing or corporate public relations programme. It helps to build a favourable attitude towards a company and its products through recognition that the company understands its business, the needs of its customers, and the marketplace.

Become a thought leader

A thought leader is a company that actively promotes and discusses ideas that are relevant to their marketplace. By talking about a topic with authority, you can become

become recognised as the leader in that field recognised as the leader in that field. As a result, the market assumes that your company has the experience and knowledge behind it to support what you are saying. If you become a thought leader in your field, it doesn't matter how big or how small your company is. Customers and prospects look to your company for insight and vision, journalists will quote you, analysts will call you and websites will link to yours.

> *Marketing secret*
>
> ◆ Thought leadership helps to build a favourable attitude towards a company and its products through recognition that the company understands its business, the needs of its customers, and the marketplace.

Most companies have to work hard to get visibility, especially in a crowded marketplace. If your reputation is not strong, you may find that prospects don't want to buy from an unknown vendor. They prefer to buy from companies they can trust with confidence. Trust is built on reputation and reputation is generally not built on advertising. By becoming an industry thought leader, you can build a strong reputation, even with limited resources. Thought leadership supports your marketing and corporate objectives to sell products, generate leads or boost share price.

Make thought leadership a strategic activity

Make thought leadership a strategic imperative for your company. Your company does not need to be a leader in sales to be considered a thought leader. However, becoming a thought leader does require work and commitment. It demands the often difficult task of looking at your company from the perspective of the world outside. Generating an ongoing effort towards thought leadership is the best way to ensure that it actually happens.

> *Marketing secret*
>
> ◆ By becoming an industry thought leader, you can build a strong reputation, even with limited resources.

The key elements of a thought leadership strategy include:

◆ press relations

◆ white papers

◆ customer magazines

◆ conference presentations

◆ executive briefing meetings

◆ event sponsorship

◆ website content

◆ podcasts

◆ webcasts

◆ blogs.

Work with the press

Relations with the press forms an important part of a thought leadership strategy. You should identify the most important writers and editors who report on your market. As well as providing them with your normal product and corporate press information, you should

keep in regular contact

keep in regular contact, offering them comments and/or articles on important issues in your industry. If a newspaper or trade magazine is running a supplement on your industry, offer articles and other content. By maintaining regular contact, your company can become a trusted source for journalists, helping to increase your visibility in the press and build your reputation.

Publish white papers

White papers and case studies are useful resources that demonstrate you understand and care about the problems that your customers are trying to solve. A white paper should therefore be a piece of information, not a sales document. A good test is to avoid mentioning your company or your product in the first half of the white paper. If prospects feel that you are trying to sell, rather than inform, the white paper becomes less valuable, and is treated as a marketing message. Your white paper should therefore review problems or needs faced by the reader, rather than describe a product or service offered by your company. You can also maintain the educational value of the paper by talking about your product in generic terms, rather than by brand name – products with these features help to overcome these issues, for example. If you take this approach, you can mention your product name at the end of the document in a 'sign-off' which is separated from the main text of the document. Make your white papers accessible. If your aim is to develop thought leadership, you want as many people to know about you as possible – visitors should not have to register to find out more about you.

Marketing secret

Around 70 per cent of information technology professionals in the USA rely on white papers to make purchasing decisions.

As they are one of the most important thought-leadership tools, white papers are discussed in more detail later in this chapter.

Produce customer magazines

You can use your customer magazine to position your company as a leader in its field. The majority of the content would be contributed by independent writers on issues of general importance to the industry. There would be minimal reference to your own products or services and any company branding would be very subtle. A customer magazine used to develop thought leadership could include different types of content such as:

◆ feature articles

◆ case studies

◆ interviews with experts or senior company executives

◆ discussion panels on important topics.

Speak at conferences

Providing quality keynote speakers at a customer event can help raise your company's profile and increase awareness. You can also achieve the same results by getting on discussion panels or conference workshops. If you are participating in an external event, organisers publish dates for submission of conference papers so make sure you are aware of those dates and provide suitable material. Again, focus on providing useful information. You are there to inform and educate, to provide a unique perspective. If your speaker is selected, promote their presentation in pre-event publicity and publish their papers in your post-event communications.

Arrange executive briefing meetings

Executive briefing meetings give you the opportunity to bring your customers up to date with new developments in your business or in your industry that might benefit them. For example, you might brief them on new technical developments or new legislation that is likely to impact on them. This type of meeting not only demonstrates your professionalism and builds thought leadership, it also helps to add value to the customer relationship.

Sponsor events

Sponsoring an event in an area where you are developing thought leadership can help to enhance your reputation by association. Depending on the type of event and its popularity, sponsorship can bring benefits.

- Builds the image of your company or product through association with an event that reflects your corporate values.

- Raises awareness of your company or product through the exposure associated with an event.

Provide useful information on your website

Your website should provide a source of useful information for customers, prospects and influencers. Your website increases in value the more people know about it and link to it.

> ### Marketing secret
>
> - The Internet has become a key medium for product research. This enables you to distribute thought leadership material to prospects in a very accessible and cost-effective way.

You should therefore include:

- copies of white papers and case studies for downloading
- bulletins on research you are carrying out
- electronic copies of your customer magazines
- copies of seminar or conference papers delivered by your own speakers
- copies of published articles or news items that demonstrate thought leadership
- details of events where your company is participating

◆ blogs commenting on industry issues

◆ archive copies of webcasts or podcasts for downloading.

Publish podcasts

A podcast is an important element in developing thought leadership. If you have experts on particular topics, you can create programmes giving advice and guidance or opinions on important industry topics. You can also host discussion groups that might include your own staff, customers, suppliers and industry consultants. The discussions could again focus on important industry topics. To create a more interactive programme, you could invite questions or feedback from customers which could be added to the podcast.

Produce webcasts

Webcasts, like podcasts, enable you to develop and publish thought leadership programmes such as discussion groups or advice and guidance via the Internet. Webcasts can also be designed to be interactive between the presenter and audience. Webcasts can include:

◆ slide presentations

◆ live video

◆ text chat for live question-and-answer sessions

◆ polls and surveys.

Create blogs

Weblogs, also known as blogs, have become a popular channel of communication in recent years, creating thought leaders in the process. Blogs can provide excellent insight into the way a company works and provide a platform for commenting on industry issues. Commentators believe that companies are now less guarded in sharing intellec-

blogs can provide excellent insight

tual property or thinking in a field. Blogging is therefore an accepted channel of open communication.

Although blogging appears to be an informal medium, planning can be important if you are using a weblog as part of your thought leadership strategy. Where possible, you should produce a publishing calendar to ensure you add new content at regular intervals. This will encourage visitors to return to your site to look for new content.

Producing white papers

As we discussed earlier in the chapter, white papers are one of the most important tools in a thought leadership programme and represent a valuable medium for communicating with both business and technical decision makers.

> *Marketing secret*
>
> ◆ White papers are particularly valuable in the early stages of purchase when decision makers are gathering information.

White papers help people make decisions. Industry research indicates that around 70 per cent of information technology professionals in the USA rely on white papers to make purchasing decisions. They are particularly valuable in the early stages of purchase when decision makers are gathering information. White papers provide information that enables readers to evaluate products, services or technologies. In the IT sector, for example, choosing the right technology has become critical to business success. Product evaluation has therefore become more intense, particularly on large-scale projects. Preparing a technical – and financial – justification is an extremely rigorous process. The detailed information available in white papers meets part of that research process, providing documentation that can guide and support decision making.

White papers fall into a number of different categories, including:

◆ **Technology guides** – Explaining a product's technology, why the technology is important to potential customers, and how it's different from and better than similar technologies.

◆ **Position papers** – Explaining a trend, or technology.

◆ **Business guides** – Explaining the business and financial benefits of a product or service.

◆ **Competitive reviews** – Evaluating a company's products and comparing them with similar competitive offerings.

◆ **Product guides** – Providing a detailed description and explanation of a product's features and functionality.

◆ **Application guides** – Describing the application of a product or technology in a particular industry.

Your white paper should have a specific objective. Possible objectives include:

- educating potential customers
- providing a response to a request for technical information
- informing decision makers of key product features or benefits
- supporting the introduction of a new technology or product feature
- educating your own salesforce or a distributor's sales team who may not fully understand your product and its benefits
- providing a background document for a press release or press conference
- creating a fulfilment piece for advertisements, direct mail or website campaigns, where readers register details to obtain a copy of the white paper.

Your white paper must have the feel of an independent, authoritative document. It should educate readers, not sell. If you use case studies to demonstrate key points, these should also be written in a 'neutral' tone that does not make marketing claims. The best white papers become recognised as authoritative sources of information that provide decision makers with an independent perspective on complex issues and challenges that they face. Wherever possible, the paper should also quote from recognised authorities in the field, such as analysts or research organisations to give further balance. In some cases, you may be able to get your white paper adopted and sponsored by a trade association or other industry body, giving it additional credibility and authority. If your company's products or services are mentioned, they should be described in neutral terms, for example, 'products such as ABC are one of a range of solutions from different vendors that can help you deal with those challenges'. The aim is to inform, not sell. It is acceptable to mention your product name at the end of the document in a 'sign-off' which is separated from the main text of the document.

Marketing secret

◆ A white paper should be a piece of information, not a sales document. A good test is to avoid mentioning your company or your product in the first half of the white paper.

Because the level of writing is so critical, you need to decide who should write the paper. Although the obvious candidate would be a technical specialist who is an expert in the subject, that person may not be capable of writing at the appropriate level. It may be more useful to appoint an editor to work with the expert, taking the expert's first draft and turning it into a document that meets the communications objectives and information needs of the target audience. The editor might be someone from your own marketing department or an independent editor/writer who is familiar with your industry. The alternative is to commission an independent writer or consultant to produce the document, working with your technical team to source and check information. If the independent writer is recognised as an authority in your industry, that can add to the credibility and objectivity of your white paper.

You should remember that white papers may also be read by non-technical readers. If communicating with business decision makers is one of your important objectives, you must ensure the content will be understandable to a non-specialist audience. Some companies produce several versions of the same paper, with a description on the front cover such as 'This publication is intended for technical readers' or 'This publication is intended for executive decisions makers'.

> *white papers may also be read by non-technical readers*

The title is an important element of a white paper. It should be informative, such as 'A guide to XYZ', but should not promise more than it can deliver. At the beginning of the document, you should include an overview and a contents list. The main body of the paper should set out the background to the paper and explain the issues and challenges facing the reader or the industry, before offering a description and justification of the solution. Depending on the subject, the paper could also include any relevant research material or case studies to support the recommendations. You should provide a summary at the end of the paper, together with a list of related documents or sources for additional information.

Because of their important role in purchasing decisions, white papers are now widely available as downloads on suppliers' websites. The Internet has become a key medium for product research and white papers are an integral part of that process. This enables you to distribute information to prospects in a very accessible and cost-effective way. You should make it easy for visitors to find your white papers:

◆ Create a library listing all the white papers available.

◆ Place links to white papers on pages where you describe relevant products or industry solutions.

◆ Place a list of white papers on your press information page.

A white paper can form a valuable mailing piece to customers and prospects. Mailing it to customers keeps them up to date with the latest developments in your company. You can also send the paper to prospects in the same market sector to demonstrate your credibility. If you are running an advertising or direct mail campaign, a white paper makes a valuable and measurable call to action. Ask readers who request the white paper to provide contact details or complete a short questionnaire, giving you useful data for later follow-up by the sales team.

Marketing secret

◆ A white paper makes a valuable and measurable call to action.

You can also distribute white papers through companies who specialise in syndicating white papers for a particular industry. These companies offer readers a wide range of material from different suppliers so that readers can compare different offerings. With syndication services, you pay the specialist to place your white paper on a network of websites that coincide with your target audience. Make sure that the syndicator can reach your targets, ideally by job title and industry (for example, if you want to reach technical managers in the printing industry). The syndicator should also be able to provide you with data that indicates how your white paper campaigns are performing. This may be simply the number of downloads, or you may get more precise information by job title or even by named company.

A little knowledge goes a long way

Thought leadership can be a powerful weapon in building your corporate reputation and adding further value to your products and services. It helps to educate your customers and to demonstrate why they should trust your company as well as your products. As we saw in the chapter on community, thought leadership can help to encourage feedback from your customers and provide valuable insight into their real needs and concerns. That makes it an essential element in brand building.

Building understanding and awareness can also be important when you are trying to gain customer acceptance for your pricing decisions, as the next chapter explains.

9

Risky business – pricing in challenging times

HOW DO YOU SET PRICES in challenging economic conditions? Competing on price alone to maintain market share may be risky. It's therefore important to retain a balance and continue concentrating on performance and quality factors that differentiate your business. By identifying the pricing factors that are important to customers, you can use that knowledge to win and retain business.

Pricing in a downturn

Challenging economic conditions mean consumer and business spending habits are changing. It's essential to recognise the trends and respond with changes to products, services and pricing that meet your customers' changing needs. Although heavy discounting can maintain cashflow, it may also damage profitability unless costs can be reduced.

> **Marketing secret**
>
> ◆ The use of heavy discounting can also create customer expectations and make it difficult to return to normal pricing when trading conditions improve.

The early stages of the recent recession saw a period of panic price cutting and 'permanent sales' as businesses tried to maintain cashflow. Heavy discounting accelerated when a number of high-profile retail chains failed, although the recession alone may not have been the main cause of failure. Before the recession, some retail chains had used permanent sales as a feature of their business. Although this may have proved a competitive advantage in normal trading conditions, it may be less of a differentiator in a recession.

In a downturn, price strategy should have two main aims – to maintain cashflow and to protect market share and customer loyalty. You can use differential pricing and discounting to reward and retain loyal or high-value customers. Loyalty pricing can also be tied to longer-term contracts for services or product supply. This kind of pricing would be appropriate for business-to-business markets where higher value customer groups can be easily identified. It may also be appropriate for consumer markets where manufacturers or retailers set up customer clubs offering members preferential discounts and other loyalty benefits.

> **Marketing secret**
>
> ◆ A selective pricing strategy rewards loyal customers, protects market share and strengthens key relationships.

Reducing prices to generate more sales will not improve your business in the long term. However, cutting costs can help to ensure survival and levels of profitability. Controlling costs and streamlining processes by reducing inefficiencies allows you to offer prices at levels your competitors cannot sustain. One way to improve efficiency and reduce costs without investment is to partner with other organisations in a business ecosystem (see Chapter 15 for details). Members of a business ecosystem can utilise their partners' skills and resources for a wide range of business functions, including sales, marketing, manufacturing, technical support and customer training. This provides a flexible, scalable business model that allows member companies to adapt their operations and lower costs in line with customer demand by using partner resources, rather than making slower, longer-term investments.

To prevent a price strategy from damaging your business, it's important to build profit contribution goals, as well as sales goals for products, market segments, and individual customers. Setting profitability goals may take precedence over market-share goals if there is a risk to the long-term viability of the business.

it's important to build profit contribution goals

Recognise customers' changing needs

How important is your product or service to your customers? If your customers are dependent on your product or service, you can base your pricing on that factor, rather than your own costs or competitors' prices. This is called 'customer value pricing'. However, the basis for customer value can change in times of recession.

◆ When economic conditions are good, customers put a higher value on products and services that give them a strong competitive advantage, for example, by improving their quality or increasing their production capacity.

◆ In a recession, the emphasis may be on products or services that ensure survival, for example by reducing their costs.

> *Marketing secret*
>
> ◆ Customer value pricing pays dividends. Even in times of recession, a customer who is dependent on a product would find it difficult to argue about price.

tailor your offer and get the best possible price

The more you understand about the problems your product solves for the customer, the easier it is to tailor your offer and get the best possible price for each sale. Even in times of recession, a customer who is dependent on a product would find it difficult to argue about price.

Although you may believe that your products are important or even essential to customers, the market may have a different perception of value. Experience indicates that, within a single marketplace, some prospects will feel that products are too expensive, while others would have continued to buy even if prices were higher. Interview your customers to find out how they view your products and services. By building a better understanding of market perceptions, you can segment and target your prices to meet different customer requirements. Any knowledge of the value you deliver to your customers gives you greater control and confidence in your pricing.

A key factor in the price relationship between you and your customers is the value you can demonstrate. When you can help customers reduce costs, improve their business performance or strengthen their competitive position, you can get closer to customers and build a dependent relationship. Presenting a product or service in this way helps to deal with low-price, low-quality competition, adds value to the product or service and positions your company as a supplier offering a strategically-important package.

Marketing secret

◆ Customers may be prepared to pay a higher price for the product or service if it makes an important contribution to their business.

Some prices can be justified on the basis of higher performance or higher value to the customer. They help the customer produce a better product or achieve a key business objective quickly or more effectively. If the product or service is unique, then naturally it warrants a premium price.

Help customers reduce their costs

'Through-life cost' is a concept used in engineering to describe products that have a value beyond their initial purchase price. For example, a component that is higher priced may be simple to assemble, easy to maintain and have a long life. The costs of that product over a whole life are likely to be lower than those of an inferior product that may cost less initially, but prove expensive in the long run when installation, servicing and replacement costs are taken into account. By working with the customer to identify and reduce through-life costs, you can identify opportunities for pricing changes.

Marketing secret

◆ The perceived value of pricing can be improved by offering customers a package of products and services that represent real value for money for their business.

Suppliers who include installation, training and initial support in the package can offer better value for money than competitors who simply sell the product to customers and expect them to meet the costs of start-up. Your customers may have to acquire new skills to install the product, set up training programmes for users and support staff, and provide a high level of support during the implementation period. To help customers handle implementation more efficiently and cost effectively, you can offer services such as carrying out initial installation and offering the services of an engineer on site to improve the skills of customer support staff and provide any specialist support needed. The prices for these services represent value for money because the customer does not have to recruit additional, costly staff.

If you have a reputation for supplying high-quality, but expensive products, you can justify the cost difference by offering the customer a level of superior reliability that they can build into their own products. This is particularly important in the components market where companies rely on supplier quality to protect their own reputation and brand image. In some markets such as information technology, component quality has become so important that many components are now strongly-branded products in their own right, as the 'Intel Inside' case in Chapter 6 demonstrates.

Major expenditure can be justified by its return on investment – how well and how quickly the expenditure pays for itself in benefits to the business. For example, a major consultancy project which improves a customer's competitive edge may be expensive, but it will pay for itself *major expenditure can be justified by its return on investment* in enhanced revenue, profitability and market share, providing a high return on investment. Products that are strategically important are more likely to provide a good return on investment than commodity products.

Deliver strategically important products

Positioning a product or service as strategically important helps to assure customers that they are buying more than a commodity. The product or service is shown to be important to the success of the customer's business and this helps to ensure it represents value for money.

> *Marketing secret*
>
> ◆ Strategically important products can help you differentiate yourself from competitors, charge higher prices and build effective relationships with customers.

Just selling a product or service does not create a strong relationship with a customer. It is the added-value benefits that increase customer dependency and provide the basis for an effective, long-term relationship. The relationship can cover a wide area of collaboration, from technical cooperation, shared manufacturing resources, joint ventures and development programmes, to shared distribution and logistics networks. The higher the level of strategic importance, the greater the dependency in the relationship.

Strategically important products have a number of characteristics:

◆ Essential to business success.

◆ Support the core business.

◆ Speed up business processes.

◆ Enable new product or market developments.

◆ Reduce the cost of key business processes.

Essential to business success

Products and services can be differentiated on the basis of their value to the business. Commodity products have little visible difference – price is similar, quality and performance equivalent, and the results similar. However, if your product or service is directly targeted at business needs, it can be clearly differentiated, and priced in line with the customer's needs. Examples include:

◆ training services to ensure customer staff get the best results from their systems

◆ project services to help customers complete essential projects faster and allow their own staff to concentrate on key business activities

◆ contract design and research services that customers can use to push their own product development programmes ahead at a faster rate, thus keeping ahead of their competitors.

Support customers' core business

Products and services provide a valuable role when they support a customer's core business. The service then becomes essential to the customer's own business. For example, if a company wanted to introduce a telemarketing programme to support its own customer relationship programmes, but didn't have the skills, facilities or resources, a specialist supplier could provide the telesales infrastructure and integrate it with the customer's own marketing activities. The customer could then concentrate on their core business development, without diverting scarce resources to handle the support activities.

Speed up customers' business processes

Speed is an essential element in markets where the pace of change puts increasing pressure on rapid product development. A company that offers new product consultancy and provides a whole range of support services will enable the customer to speed up product development. Customers can get new products to market or introduce new services more quickly without committing their own resources. Getting there quicker means that they can stay ahead of the competition and improve their response to changing market conditions – both essential to maintaining long-term turnover and profitability.

Enable new developments

Sometimes companies are prevented from exploiting profitable new developments because they lack the skills or resources needed for success. By filling that gap in the customer's resources and demonstrating how it can be used to provide a strategy for growth, you can position your services as strategically important. By providing these scarce skills to supplement the customer's own resources, you can help the customer develop and introduce the new products rapidly. The customer will be able to compete effectively while continuing to concentrate on their core business. Your pricing is then based on increasing levels of customer dependency.

Reduce cost of business processes

Customers also benefit from a reduction in the cost of their business processes. Using their own staff to handle everything can be expensive because certain skills may be used only occasionally. By analysing all their activities and dividing them into core and non-core activities, you can decide where support will be beneficial. The support services they buy in are strategically important. If you have the skilled staff and the infrastructure to deliver the service cost effectively, you can reduce the overall cost of your customers' business processes.

Manage your pricing

By recognising your customers' changing needs and assessing levels of dependency, you can offer different groups a range of prices or price packages for the same basic product. For example, you could offer 'first-class' or 'economy' prices. First-class customers receive extra value, such as faster delivery or complementary services by paying a premium price. Economy customers pay *price segmentation can help you reach different markets* a lower price but would get just the basic product, with no added value. This type of price segmentation can help you reach different markets without changing the specification or costs of your basic product.

While it may be important to offer a competitive 'headline price', you should also consider opportunities to maintain profitability by recovering some of the costs involved in order processing, delivery, financing or other customer-facing processes:

◆ Set minimum order quantities to minimise order processing costs.

◆ Focus on collection efforts to improve cashflow.

◆ Offer customers a priced menu of essential services such as delivery or preferential discounts.

◆ Identify opportunities for incremental sales of value-added services such as consultancy, planning, installation, training and maintenance.

◆ Offer preferential discounts for long-term contracts to smooth out revenue.

By charging separately for these type of services, it is possible to offset the potential loss of both income and profit created by a price reduction.

Marketing secret

◆ A good pricing strategy recognises the importance of protecting strong brands.

During a recession, a better strategy is to keep high-value products priced appropriately, but focus on selling more low-value products and services. Using price cuts to maintain business on high-value products or eroding margins by giving away services or offering discounts to customers can prove a false economy. Price cuts can erode the base of profitable customers and reduce the potential for profitability when the downturn ends.

In a recession, revenue losses can occur because the salesforce or retail network finds it difficult to resist customer pressure for price cuts. Sales teams may find themselves lowering prices to ensure they win the sale – at any cost. To discourage or prevent this, it is important to impose business rules that relate price negotiations to different volume, delivery, financing and settlement criteria.

The business rules should also reflect the value of the product or service to the customer. To reinforce the business rules, it may be necessary to change the basis of salesforce compensation to reflect the contribution to profitability and customer retention, rather than pure sales volume.

Plan for a return to growth

Although an effective pricing strategy can help to maintain revenue and profitability, it's also important to continue investment in marketing. Typically in a recession, marketing budgets are cut in an effort to boost quarterly performance. However, with reducing demand and increasing competition, this could prove counterproductive. Industry research indicates that maintaining or increasing marketing during a recession can strengthen a company's position in the short to medium term, and in the longer term as the economy picks up. Continuing to invest in marketing will provide you with a number of benefits:

◆ If competitors reduce their marketing, there is less 'noise' to compete with and campaigns will gain a louder, clearer voice.

◆ Customers respond to suppliers who are still actively engaging with them, and delivering messages that are relevant to their changing needs. If brand awareness falls, market share is also likely to go down and that may be hard to win back.

◆ When customers spend less, every sale will be harder to win. Companies who continue to invest in marketing bring stronger resources to the fight.

In many companies, marketing is perceived as a variable cost that can be cut without harming sales. This runs contrary to industry experience, so it is important to convince budget holders that marketing is a revenue generator, and an essential activity for survival and future growth. Combined with a flexible, realistic price strategy, investment in marketing can deliver profitable results.

> *Marketing secret*
>
> ◆ The right pricing strategies will not only strengthen business in a downturn, it will also position you for growth later in normal trading conditions.

Companies with a strong brand image ensure that a 'survival' pricing strategy will not cheapen the long-term value of their product. They recognise that customers will not automatically accept a return to higher prices in the future, but they also realise that customers will respond to a value message that is directly relevant to them.

The price is right

Pricing decisions are always difficult, but more so in an economic downturn. Communicating price-related benefits that customers may not be aware of can help to build acceptance for price changes and help to build dependency. Even if your company has a reputation for high pricing, you can use that to your advantage by demonstrating that quality pays for itself in the long term. Buying low-price products might save the customer money initially, but add in maintenance and replacement costs later and the savings won't look so good. What you are offering the customer is a great overall package and that can help to overcome any price challenges.

Pricing messages are an important part of an overall communications strategy. The next section explains other ways to build preference for your company.

PART 3

Don't keep it secret: get the story across

This section looks at the importance of marketing communications, including who to target and what to say. It explains the importance of communicating corporate information, as well as product details and describes how integrating communications can pay real bonuses in terms of effectiveness, cost and impact.

10 How to win friends and influence the influencers

Do you know who really makes the decision to buy your products, and who influences them? In many cases, it isn't just the front-line prospect who warrants your attention and marketing budget. Purchasing managers consult technical managers, finance directors and other board executives as part of their decision-making process. Are you reaching all the people who matter, and do you know what they think of you and your competitors?

11 Trust me, I'm financially sound

You might run successful campaigns, have market-leading products and a dynamic salesforce, but if customers don't have confidence in your long-term financial stability, your market share could evaporate rapidly. Make sure your marketing communications describe your business and financial strengths, as well as your technical capability.

12 How many agencies does it take to change a prospect's mind?

Advertising agencies handle advertising, PR consultancies manage media relations, design groups produce the brochures, Internet companies develop the online campaigns and website ... the list goes on. In theory, they are focusing on the same target audience, but are they always communicating the same messages and brand values? By using so many different agencies, are costs being duplicated? Using just one integrated agency can improve your marketing performance by ensuring consistent messaging in every communication – and save you money. Using a technique called 'joined-up marketing' can bring even greater benefits.

10

How to win friends and influence the influencers

DO YOU KNOW WHO REALLY makes the decision to buy your products, and who influences them? In many cases, it isn't just the front-line prospect who warrants your attention and marketing budget. Purchasing managers consult technical managers, finance directors and other board executives as part of their decision-making process. Are you reaching all the people who matter, and do you know what they think of you and your competitors?

Communicate at the right level

In business purchasing, more than one person influences the choice of supplier. A decision-making team could include a wide range of key personnel, and the influence of team members varies at different stages during the purchasing process. It is important to identify the members of the team and communicate with each at the appropriate stage.

You need to find out who within your customer's company is interested in your products. Telephone research, direct mail, or advertising with a response mechanism can help to identify other team members.

Marketing secret

◆ Be careful about direct approaches to decision makers: purchasing managers may guard their status and resent approaches to other team members that appear to be undermining their position.

Suppose your company sells low-value commodity components. Do you need to identify a complete decision-making team? On the surface, your task should be simple. Just deal with the person who orders the products. However, there may be bigger opportunities. The technical manager may not be happy with the performance of commodity products. The research team or the marketing department may be planning new products, which could change the product specification. You need to monitor changing customer requirements.

You may already recognise that your company needs to talk to senior directors about the strategic importance of your products. How can you do this when your sales team never gets the opportunity to meet directors? It is unlikely that directors would have time during the normal working day to meet sales representatives, or regard a sales meeting as high on their list of priorities. You could arrange a seminar or executive briefing session that would appeal to directors. That would ensure you meet the right people and give you the opportunity to find out more about their needs.

ensure you meet the right people

These are some of the challenges you face when you're planning a communications programme. Target the wrong people and you could be wasting your budget.

Identify the decision makers

At a simple level, there are just two types of people involved in a business purchase decision. The identification of the need is usually the responsibility of a business decision maker. They pass the business requirement to the technical decision maker for solution research, design and evaluation. The solution then goes back to the business decision maker for approval and purchase. To move companies through the buying cycle, you therefore need to influence two main audiences.

The business decision maker They are driven by business growth and competitive pressure, and they face comparison with their peers. They look for solutions to business pain points. However, they may not have any technical knowledge and they may not be aware of your company.

The technical decision maker They may be familiar with your company but may not be aware of all your products. You need to help them understand how different products work and provide examples of how solutions could be deployed to drive business benefits.

However, in reality, many other people influence the choice of supplier. Individuals make different contributions to the decision-making process and they usually have different information requirements.

> *Marketing secret*
>
> ◆ Many companies have adopted team purchasing structures to deal with high-value purchases and it is important that you communicate effectively with every member of the team.

Decision-making teams

Depending on the value and complexity of the purchase, a decision-making team could include:

◆ senior executives

◆ purchasing professionals

◆ technical staff

◆ manufacturing managers

◆ marketing staff

◆ departmental managers.

As a rough guideline, you are likely to be dealing with a powerful purchasing organisation if any of the following conditions apply:

◆ Your product is a vital component, or strategically important to your customers.

- Your product is technically complex.

- Your product is of high value.

If your product is of relatively low value, purchasing decisions are more likely to revolve around price and delivery, and it is unlikely that a team would be involved.

The influence of team members varies at different stages during the purchasing process:

- Purchasing staff and departmental managers may have considerable early influence when a specification is being drawn up.

- When proposals are being evaluated, technical staff may be more influential.

- Senior business executives are unlikely to be interested in detail, but they will need an overview of the overall business benefits of the product or service.

> *Marketing secret*
> - The influence of decision makers varies at different stages during the purchasing process.

Senior executives

Senior executives need an overview of the business benefits of a product or service, and seek reassurance that your organisation is capable of supplying their long-term needs – any risk could be detrimental to their own business. Many suppliers try to move discussion of their products and services to board level to demonstrate that they are of strategic importance. This can be a useful exercise in developing business, because it can build a level of dependency that is important to account control.

Purchasing professionals

Purchasing professionals are usually the key figures in a purchasing team. While they may not take sole responsibility for decision making, they are likely to be the team leaders and will remain your main point of contact. Many companies operate a preferred supplier programme and, to be recognised, you may have to meet a detailed list of criteria. The purchasing department is instrumental in managing the list of approved suppliers. Many of the preferred supplier programmes include rating schemes to measure suppliers' performance; these are part of a process of developing effective relationships, so that purchasing professionals can provide an even better service to their internal customers.

Finance executives

Finance executives have ultimate control over purchasing budgets, and they're likely to be involved if purchases are complex or entail major capital expenditure.

improve your competitive position by offering flexible schemes

They seek reassurance that they are getting value for money and that their purchase represents the best return on investment. They may consider alternative methods of financing, and you may be able to improve your competitive position by offering flexible schemes such as leasing or deferred payments.

Technical staff

Technical staff are a vital part of the purchasing team. They are responsible for improving the performance of the company products in order to develop a competitive edge. You therefore need to be closely involved with the technical team at a number of stages. When they are developing new products, you should be involved at the planning stages so you can influence the design. When they are enhancing existing products, you should be developing proposals to improve product performance. If they are moving into new markets, you can support them by handling contract development services, or by training their staff. You can provide them with a range of specialist technical services that enable them to provide a better service to their internal customers.

Manufacturing managers

If you are introducing an innovative product, or you have identified an opportunity to improve your customers' manufacturing operations or reduce costs, you need to influence manufacturing specialists.

Marketing staff

Marketing specialists ensure that a product or service adds value and helps the company to develop a stronger competitive position. They will play an important part in decision making if your customers are seeking to improve their market position or are entering new markets where you have a specific expertise.

Departmental managers

Departmental managers are often the users of your products or services. They need to be reassured that they will benefit from dealing with a particular supplier. They play an important role in specifying the product and evaluating the performance of existing suppliers.

Research decision makers

Although it is simple to list potential decision makers, it is more complicated to identify who is actually involved in the process.

Marketing secret

◆ Many decision makers may not have a direct role in a project team, or may be involved in only part of the purchasing process. Don't overlook them.

Many decision makers may not have a direct role in a project team, or may be involved in only part of the purchasing process, so you need to look carefully at your research processes. Your sales team in regular contact with the customer should be best placed to identify the key decision makers. There are a number of other techniques for identifying other influencers:

◆ Independent research into how companies buy different types of product or service; the survey may be limited to a specific group of customers, or carried out across a whole industry.

- Published industry surveys on buying patterns; these provide broad guidelines to the key decision makers but need to be qualified by specific account research.

- Direct response advertising, in which responses are analysed to identify decision-making patterns.

- Joint projects, in which members of the customer team work with members of your team; the relationships and approval procedures that emerge provide useful clues about who are the hidden decision makers.

Research like this should be carried out continuously because purchasing is a dynamic activity. Members of the decision-making team may change their jobs and, as the process progresses, individual contributions change.

> *purchasing is a dynamic activity*

Concentrate on the right people

Don't focus your sales team on the wrong decision makers. Companies rarely make it clear who influences the purchasing decisions. Meetings with the purchasing manager could be wasted if someone else draws up the specification. If it is an innovative component that enables them to develop a new product or enter new markets, your company then becomes a potential strategic partner.

Marketing secret

- You may think you are just selling your customers a product or a service, but your product may make an important contribution to their business.

Make sure that you communicate this to the right people – the senior decision makers, not the person who simply issues the purchase orders. Purchasing requirements change and so do the people who make the decisions. Customers may launch new products, drop old ones, or acquire other companies. People come and go, and that influences the structure of the decision-making team. Make sure you keep up to date with the latest developments.

keep up to date with the latest developments

Plan the campaign cycle

Every sales prospect goes through a 'customer journey', moving from a prospect with little or no awareness of a company and its products to a loyal customer placing high levels of repeat business. At each stage of the journey, companies can use specific marketing tools and activities to engage prospects and communicate with them effectively. This is known as the campaign cycle and includes five main stages – raising awareness, driving consideration, reinforcing preference, purchase and building loyalty. Companies rarely buy products or services on impulse. The decision to buy is the result of a long process of investigation, consideration and review. Different people will evaluate products and companies. To be able to market and sell effectively and to make the best use of your marketing resources, it's important to understand how your customers and prospects buy, and to recognise which stage of the cycle they are currently in.

> *Marketing secret*
>
> ◆ Companies rarely buy products or services on impulse.
> The decision to buy is the result of a long process of
> investigation, consideration and review.

Although your customers and prospects may vary in size, most companies share a common buying cycle. This can help you determine the nature of your marketing campaign. The buying cycle typically moves through four key stages:

1 Identify a business need.

2 Research a solution.

3 Design and evaluate different solutions.

4 Purchase.

Decision makers need different types of information at different stages of the buying cycle. When they are first investigating a business need, they may not be familiar with your company or understand how your products and services meet their needs. Later, when they are close to purchase, they may need reassurance that your company is capable of delivering on its promises. It's important that you match those different information needs with the right communications at the right time.

> *Marketing secrets*
>
> ◆ Decision makers need different types of information at
> different stages of the buying cycle.

Understanding your prospective customer's buying cycle also helps to highlight who makes the decisions at each stage of the cycle. Your advertisements may be aimed at the wrong decision makers, or your sales teams may be contacting prospects at the wrong level. Wrong targeting wastes money and may lose you opportunities to win business.

Your marketing campaigns need to target the different levels of awareness and readiness to buy at different stages of the buying cycle. When your prospects are identifying a business need, you need to:

◆ raise awareness of your company and its products

◆ demonstrate the relevance of your products to the business need.

When the prospect is researching a solution, you need to:

◆ continue raising awareness of your company and its products

◆ continue demonstrating the relevance of your products to the business need

◆ nurture the relationship with your prospect

◆ encourage consideration of your product.

When the prospect is designing and evaluating different solutions, you need to:

◆ continue nurturing the relationship with your prospect

◆ build preference for your product.

When the prospect is ready to purchase, you need to:

◆ reinforce preference for your product

◆ make it easy for the prospect to purchase your product.

To identify the prospect's key objectives, you need to:

◆ review focus group research and transcripts

◆ review research articles or reports in business publications/user groups

◆ consider setting up an online poll.

Set campaign objectives

Your campaign should be designed to support your revenue growth goals and the specific needs of your business strategy. The campaign should focus on two important marketing objectives:

◆ Increase the number of new customers.

◆ Increase the number of repeat customers.

These, in turn, drive the communication objectives and strategy. To align with the buying cycle, your communications should have three specific objectives:

1 **New contact acquisition** – To drive awareness and relevance of your company and your products.

2 **Relationship marketing** – To develop deeper customer insight and strengthen relationships. Your aim is to move from a transactional approach to a relationship marketing approach. You should nurture new contacts

and develop a trusted advisor relationship for your company and your channel partners.

3 **Lead generation** – To drive consideration and preference for your solutions. You can run a variety of lead generation programmes to drive preference for your products.

Run a new contact acquisition programme

The aim of the acquisition programme is to attract new contacts and prospects by making them aware of your company and demonstrating the business relevance of your products and services. To do this, communications should focus on the key pain points and concerns of decision makers, and demonstrate the value you have brought to similar companies. The main focus of the communication programme is on public relations and online activities. These could include:

◆ public relations stories relating to business pain points

◆ customer success stories in print and video format

◆ online web banners with a business and technology focus

◆ web pages with business and technology sections

◆ print advertisements.

The key measurement for this programme is the number of new contacts.

Run a relationship marketing programme

The aims of the relationship marketing programme are to:

◆ acquire and nurture new contacts

◆ strengthen relationships with existing customers.

A programme of regular newsletters and other information can provide a communication platform for ongoing regular communication with customers and prospects. Newsletter content should follow the structure of the main campaign with articles to support both business and technology themes.

The key measurements are numbers of new contacts and percentage response rates.

Increase lead generation

As well as providing immediate sales leads, a lead generation programme can help to identify new contacts and information on future purchase plans that can be used in subsequent marketing activities. The programme could include:

♦ communications templates for telemarketing scripts, email, direct mail

♦ customer offers including event invitations and demonstrations

♦ supporting collateral including press release templates, how to sell guides, white papers and customer presentations.

The key measurements are conversion rate of leads to customers, number of new customers and number of repeat purchases.

Decisions, decisions ...

Life was simple when buying was left to the purchasing manager, but now your challenge is to influence a whole team of people who are involved in the purchase decision.

Who are they and how important are they to the final decision? To succeed, you need to understand their concerns and challenges and you need to know when they are involved in the decision-making process. Get that right and you'll be able to operate a targeted communications programme that moves your prospects towards a positive decision.

For some members of a decision-making team, trust and confidence in a supplier is a critical element. The next chapter explains how to build that confidence.

11

Trust me, I'm financially sound

YOU MIGHT RUN successful campaigns, have market-leading products and a dynamic salesforce, but if customers don't have confidence in your long-term financial stability, your market share could evaporate rapidly. Make sure your marketing communications describe your business and financial strengths, as well as your technical capability.

Build confidence in your company

It's important to build confidence in your company as a stable long-term supplier, committed to quality rather than price, with a sound management structure and growth opportunities in its chosen markets. Financial stability not only influences your ability to compete; it can also give your management team access to the funds needed for further growth. Presenting a company as financially stable can have a number of important benefits:

◆ It reassures customers that you are a reliable supplier.

◆ It can help you win long-term contracts.

◆ It can provide you with access to funds.

◆ It tells current and prospective employees that your company has good long-term prospects.

If your company has a poor reputation in the market, can corporate communications overcome that? It is always important to correct wrong perceptions, but if the perceptions are based on poor performance, the focus should be on improving the performance itself. Trying to mislead the market can be dangerous.

Marketing secret

◆ Corporate communications can help to correct wrong perceptions, but the real focus should be on improving your company's performance.

If, on the other hand, your company's products have an excellent reputation in the market, why should you worry about corporate communications? Success depends on more than a good product range. Your company may have excellent products but a poor delivery record. If demand is growing, customers will ask if you have the capacity to meet new levels of demand. If your company is not making good profits, customers will ask whether it can invest for the future or even survive in the long term.

keep customers informed about your company

These are good reasons to keep customers informed about your company.

Corporate communications can be important in a number of different business scenarios:

◆ Your company has recently undergone significant change.

◆ Research shows that customers are not aware of your company's key strengths.

◆ Your company is entering new markets and there is low awareness among potential customers.

◆ Research shows that the company has a poor reputation in a number of areas important to its success.

◆ Purchasing decisions are influenced by executives who are not aware of the company.

◆ Your company is trying to build partnership relationships and customers need to know that you are capable of providing stable supply.

Identify the elements of your reputation

Your corporate reputation is the way your company is perceived by customers, suppliers and other important groups. It is based on a number of elements, including:

◆ financial performance

◆ quality of the management team

◆ clarity of direction

◆ market performance

◆ growth record and potential

◆ relationships with suppliers and employees

◆ manufacturing capability.

The first stage in building a positive corporate reputation is to assess current perceptions of the organisation through research. This is the management summary of one company's research into customer perceptions:

◆ The company is almost as 'visible' as its competitors, but is rated only third in all issues associated with image.

◆ Contact with the customer at all levels is less than professional. According to the customer, the company does not understand its business and its products, and does not communicate its future strategies.

◆ There is a legacy of poor reputation which has largely been overcome by increased product reliability, but the image persists in the minds of the customer's senior management team.

◆ The company is perceived as offering lower quality and lower performance than competitors, and users are less satisfied than competitive users.

◆ The company is seen as losing ground with important decision makers.

◆ The company is identified more clearly than competitors with specific product lines, but is not rated most highly as the potential supplier of those products.

◆ The company's major weakness is perceived as its narrow product line and lack of expertise in certain areas.

Keep your customers up to date

An audit similar to the one above identifies key areas for improving communications performance. It is essential that key messages are consistently communicated in every form of contact with your customers. Significant developments such as new investment programmes, acquisitions, changes in management, expansion programmes or new product launches are of major interest to your customers. Take the opportunity to update everyone on progress.

it is essential that key messages are consistently communicated

---

Marketing secret

◆ Customers need to understand your company's future direction as well as your current status as a supplier.

It is also important that your customers understand the future direction of your company – how you see your business in the medium and long term, what new developments you plan to introduce, and any fundamental changes to your business that you may be considering. They need to be convinced that you will remain committed to the success of their business and that they will continue to benefit from working closely with you. An understanding of your future direction helps your customers plan their own development.

To help you present a complete picture of your current and future capability, this extended example illustrates the areas your communications programme could cover, such as:

- sound company structure
- serving growing markets
- sound financial controls
- strong investment record
- share price performance
- stable customer base
- broadly-based product portfolio
- record of profitability
- low cost base.

Sound company structure

Your company structure can help to reassure customers that your company will remain a reliable supplier. Customers need to know that you have the resources to finance work in progress, and that you have access to funds for research and investment for growth. In this example, the backing of a major group provides the right credentials.

Example: *The company is a key member of an international services group with offices throughout Europe. The group is one of the most successful services organisations and has an enviable record of growth and profitability. The group spends a significant proportion of its income on research and development and investment in sophisticated service tools. As a member of the group, we share the commitment to investment in service excellence.*

Serving growing markets

As well a sound structure, you can also point to market success as an indicator of good long-term prospects. For example, a company operating in sectors in overall decline, such as steel making or ship building, is unlikely to have the same long-term prospects as companies in the high-technology sector.

Example: *Our main market is services for high technology industries and we have built up effective long-term working relationships with our key clients. Eight of our top ten clients have growth rates in excess of the industry best and that provides excellent growth rates for our own business.*

Sound financial controls

Poor financial controls can bring down the most successful and profitable company and customers need reassurance that you can look after your own affairs as well as their business.

Example: *We have recently invested in a sophisticated new financial control system so that we can control our business effectively. It also helps us to provide you with a prompt billing and reporting service so that you have up-to-date information on your own finances.*

Strong investment record

A strong investment record not only shows that your company is financially sound, it also demonstrates that you are committed to providing increasingly higher standards of service. That, in turn, improves your long-term growth prospects. Investment does not necessarily mean capital expenditure on equipment; investment in people is seen as an increasingly important area for corporate development, for example.

Example: *We believe that our outstanding growth record can be attributed to consistently high levels of investment in people and in systems. Our aim is to deliver a quality service, and we do that by developing quality people. Our staff training programmes regularly win training industry awards and we are backing our people with a sophisticated service infrastructure. The combination of quality people and sophisticated tools means that we can deliver the highest standards of service and maintain high levels of market share.*

Share price performance

Customers with demanding supply requirements need to know that their suppliers can grow with them as their needs change. If a supplier does not have access to funds, they are unlikely to be able to carry out investment programmes or hire additional staff to handle higher volumes of work. Public companies therefore place a great deal of emphasis on their share price because that influences investors and can determine whether an application for funds will succeed.

Example: *The company has just completed a major reorganisation and is now set for further growth in its chosen markets. We have carried out a comprehensive training programme to equip our staff with the skills to succeed and we are setting up new control systems to manage the higher levels of business. To achieve and maintain leadership in our chosen sector, we need to invest in sophisticated service tools and we wish to fund this through a rights issue. You will see from this review of our share price over the last three years* *that we have performed consistently well and prospects for the next six months are excellent.*

Stable customer base

When you analyse your customer base, you generally find that there is a split between regular long-term customers and customers who buy occasionally and change suppliers regularly. A stable customer base which includes a high proportion of long-term customers not only indicates sound business relationships, but also says to customers that your company can provide a consistently high standard of service over a long period of time.

Example: *We build long-term relationships with our clients so that we can grow with their business and meet their changing requirements. A high percentage of our turnover is repeat business and we have a growing number of customers who have been working with us for more than five years. We are taking further steps to strengthen our relationships with key accounts so that we can predict our future growth path with greater certainty.*

Broadly-based product portfolio

As well as a stable customer base, you also need to show that your product range meets current requirements and can be developed in response to changing market conditions. The product range should contain a good balance of market-leading established products and new products with good growth potential.

Example: *Our product range covers all the key service sectors and includes products which are market leaders in the finance, defence* and transport sectors. *These products are continually refreshed with new features and we are developing new customised versions to enable us to compete effectively in other sectors. Our new product development programme has provided a regular stream of highly successful products and we are continuing to invest in our portfolio.*

Record of profitability

Profitability is a good indicator of a company's financial performance and sends the right signals to investors, employees and customers. A profitable company is generally a well-managed company and that provides the right degree of reassurance.

Example: *In a sector which is generally regarded as difficult and unprofitable, our company has consistently turned in a profitable performance. This is due, not only to our low cost base, but also to our strong market performance and our performance in account control. We have a strong management team and good relationships with the financial community. With trading conditions now extremely good, we look forward to another successful year.*

Low cost base

If your company is a high cost producer, this may affect your ability to generate profits for future growth, and your competitive ability may be damaged by low-price rivals. It is important to stress the actions that are taken to reduce costs because lower costs give your company greater flexibility and enable it to compete effectively.

Example: *We have recently carried out a major cost reduction exercise to ensure that we can compete effectively. This exercise will* not, however, affect our commitment to quality or our new product development programme. The exercise has concentrated on equipping staff with new skills and introducing sophisticated support tools to help speed up both routine and complex tasks. We are cutting our resources only in areas where there is low growth potential.

Build a positive corporate reputation

As the above extended example shows, corporate communications stress the positive aspects of your company and seek to correct any misunderstandings. By looking at the factors that are important to your customers, you can help to build their confidence and trust.

Marketing secret

◆ Corporate communications build confidence and trust with your customers.

Earlier in the chapter, we looked at one company's research into customer perceptions. Here's an example of how a company could shape up with a positive reputation in the eyes of its customers:

◆ The company is financially sound. It has the stability and financial strength to grow in line with our own increasing demands.

◆ The company is well managed. It has a dynamic management team committed to customer service and it attracts talented executives in every discipline.

◆ The company has a clear sense of direction. It is committed to market leadership and technical excellence. Its long-term product plans will help us to improve our own business performance.

◆ The company is a market leader and sets the standard for the rest of the industry. It's attracting customers who demand the highest standards of service.

◆ The company has an exciting new product range. It's clearly capable of innovation, and partnership with it will clearly benefit our organisation.

◆ The company cares for its employees. It spends a great deal on training and personal development and that is reflected in a commitment to quality.

◆ The company has an excellent investment record. Its factories are highly productive and that means quality production with good costs.

Most customers would feel confident in a supplier like that. They could trust their supplier not to let them down on quality and reliability and they could expect the supplier to help them push their own business forward. That's the kind of reputation you can aspire to.

Confidence counts

The recent economic downturn has put an even greater focus on stability. When customers are making major purchasing decisions, one of the first questions they ask is 'Will that supplier still be in business in five years' time?' This is important because the customer's own business depends on working with suppliers who understand their needs and can meet their requirements over the long term. So confidence really matters.

Corporate communications are an important tool for building confidence in your company. However, they are just part of the overall communications mix and it's important that all of the elements are integrated, with consistent messaging to your customers and prospects. The next chapter looks at the agencies who provide communications services, examining ways in which you can get better results from your agencies through integration.

confidence really matters

12

How many agencies does it take to change a prospect's mind?

ADVERTISING AGENCIES handle advertising, PR consultancies manage media relations, design groups produce the brochures, Internet companies develop online campaigns and websites ... the list goes on. In theory, they are focusing on the same target audience, but are they always communicating the same messages and brand values? By using so many different agencies, are costs being duplicated? Appointing just one integrated agency can improve your marketing performance by ensuring consistent messaging in every communication – and save you money. Using a technique called 'joined-up marketing' can bring even greater benefits.

Is integration right for your business?

Integrated marketing communications offers important creative and cost benefits, but it must be carefully evaluated before you make a commitment to a single agency solution.

These are some of the indicators that demonstrate the need for an integrated approach:

♦ Customers receive communications material from different sources in the same company.

♦ Different company departments commission their own marketing materials.

♦ Visual and copy standards vary between departments and campaigns.

♦ You are losing opportunities to cross-sell and build long-term relationships with customers.

♦ You use many different suppliers to produce marketing support material and there is little coordination between suppliers.

♦ You use many different sales channels to market your products, and channel performance varies considerably.

♦ The cost of marketing administration is high because of the number of different suppliers.

Achieve creative integrity

When a consumer gets a range of messages from the same company, they should be consistent. In just one campaign, a consumer might view a television commercial, read a press advertisement, visit the website, receive a direct mail shot, visit a retail outlet where there is point-of-sale material, pick up a product leaflet and participate in an incentive programme. At the same time, the consumer might talk to members of the salesforce, visit an exhibition and receive a call from a telemarketing specialist.

What happens if the creative treatment of each of these is different? Confusion, lack of impact. Will the consumer know that they are dealing with the same company? Each of these elements reinforces each other. While it is not essential for the visual and copy treatment to be exactly the same on each element of the campaign, they must tell the same story. A consistent build-up like this reinforces the impact of the other elements of the programme and helps to move the consumer towards a purchasing decision.

each of these elements reinforces each other

> *Marketing secret*
>
> ◆ Integration reinforces the individual elements of a marketing campaign, consistently moving customers towards a purchasing decision.

In business-to-business marketing, the scenario can be multiplied by the number of people in the decision-making process: executive briefing for the senior management team; management guides for departmental managers who might use the product; capability presentations for the buying team; technical literature for technical specialists; product literature for the purchasing department; corporate advertisements and financial public relations aimed at the important influencers; direct marketing to other members of the purchasing team; sales presentations; videos; and product proposals. Add the information that distributors and other influencers need – in the form of retail advertisements and mailers, point-of-sale material and distributor training – and the picture becomes very complex.

Integrated marketing offers strategic and creative integrity across all media. In practical terms, that means the themes and style of advertising are followed consistently through all media. If you produce many different campaigns, publications and other marketing support material for a large product range, you will be able to introduce consistent creative and visual standards.

integrated marketing offers strategic and creative integrity across all media

> ### Marketing secret
>
> ◆ Integrated marketing enables you to present a strong, unified identity and support all your products and services with powerful, consistent branding.

Make your messages consistent

In integrated marketing, all copy is written or edited centrally. Although technical information will vary by product or service, each publication, campaign or marketing communication will include 'positioning' messages that stress generic customer benefits such as quality of service, customer focus, corporate strength and other key factors. This consistency is impossible when copy is produced separately for advertisements, direct mail, product literature – all aimed at the same customer.

Visual standards also help to reinforce the consistency of integrated communications. By imposing corporate design

> **Marketing secret**
> ◆ Integrated marketing will ensure that every form of
> customer contact reinforces the customer's positive
> perception of the company.

standards on all promotional material and utilising key
visual elements on advertisements and all other communications material, a company can reinforce the visual identity.
A corporate identity is a major investment for any company,
but it pays for itself in increased recognition and stronger
perceptions. Integrated marketing reinforces the benefits of
a corporate identity programme by applying it to all media
and ensuring that the company is immediately recognised.
Different products, different campaigns and information
from separate divisions can all be coordinated by introducing
consistent messages.

Get unbiased media recommendations

If you approached an advertising agency or public relations consultancy, you would probably be surprised if they
didn't recommend media advertising or a public relations
campaign. If you briefed a design consultancy on your communication requirements, the chances are that you would
be operating a print-based programme. The more specific
the supplier, the more likely you are to get a predictable
response. This is not a criticism – it is the role of a specialist
to provide a specialised service.

However, in integrated marketing, one agency should
handle all aspects of marketing and operate 'through-the-line'.

An agency that works through-the-line has no bias towards any particular media; they are all treated with the same attention, because an integrated agency does not have to worry about earning commission. This means that the agency is able to recommend the most appropriate strategy, which might include direct marketing, incentives or sales support for distributors and agents.

Marketing secret

◆ In an integrated strategy, every element of the marketing mix is working hard and contributing to the success of the campaign.

Advertisements alone, for example, may not reach all the key decision makers for a product. Salesforce contact may be vital to securing a major contract. An extended video could provide a vital live action demonstration of the product and give the direct salesforce an important training tool. The success of a campaign may depend on effective local marketing by a distributor network. An integrated marketing agency handles the full range of communication tasks and is in a unique position to offer unbiased advice on the solution that is best for the marketing task.

In integrated marketing, different techniques and media are used to support each other to improve marketing effectiveness. For example:

◆ Direct marketing and telemarketing are used to support direct response advertising campaigns.

◆ Selected customer incentives are used to increase response to advertising or direct marketing campaigns.

◆ Relationship marketing programmes are used to increase customer retention.

◆ Sales training, targeted incentive programmes and direct marketing are used to improve direct sales performance.

Integrated marketing ensures that each medium is used to its best advantage. An exhibition specialist, for example, would be in the best position to produce a high-quality exhibition stand, but might not have the resources or the experience to supply all the back-up services that are needed to make the exhibition successful. Direct marketing of invitations to delegates and follow-up by telephone of all attendees can help to reinforce the work that was done on the stand. Incentives during the exhibition and suitable exhibition literature can all help to make the exhibition work much harder.

A seminar that is integrated with an executive briefing programme, and a direct marketing campaign that provides senior executives with useful product and service management guides ensure that *increase the impact* clients get full benefit from the seminar *and effectiveness of* and also that the communications effect *every campaign* is much stronger. By integrating editorial publicity with advertising and using telemarketing to follow up all direct marketing campaigns, you increase the impact and effectiveness of every campaign.

Achieve greater marketing precision

Integrated marketing contributes to greater marketing precision. In an integrated marketing programme, direct mail and other precision marketing tools are used extensively to achieve specific communication objectives. For example, a programme that requires consistent nationwide retail performance must include local marketing activities – product training for distributors, retail support programmes, local advertising and staff incentives to ensure commitment. Provided these activities are given professional support within an integrated marketing programme, they can be used to achieve specific, measurable objectives.

Integrated marketing makes extensive use of database marketing techniques: information from direct response advertising, direct marketing campaigns and telemarketing is used to build up a comprehensive picture of individual customers and prospects, so that future marketing programmes are focused with great precision.

The development of personalisation techniques means that marketing through a website can offer even higher levels of precision. Using information that customers supply when they register for an offer, companies can build personal web pages or plan regular email campaigns that offer individual prospects tailored information.

A single medium strategy may be concentrated on a key part of the target audience, but it runs the risk of missing the important prospects and attempting to do everything.

> *Marketing secret*
>
> ◆ Integrated marketing allows you to concentrate on your
> mainstream marketing programmes while introducing
> niche market programmes and focusing on specific
> elements of the marketing mix to win key prospects.

Improve operational efficiency

Another major benefit of integrated marketing is operational
efficiency. It takes fewer people to manage integrated marketing. There is a single point of contact with one agency,
which ties up less of your management and administrative
time. Because there is a single point of contact, there is no
inter-agency conflict of interest. When
differing departments or individuals are *there is no inter-*
working with separate specialist agencies, *agency conflict of*
there can be little coordination and a great *interest*
deal of duplication of effort. Agency and
supplier management costs are duplicated because each
agency/client relationship requires separate estimating,
ordering, invoicing and other control procedures.

> *Marketing secret*
>
> ◆ It takes fewer people to manage integrated marketing.
> By having a single point of contact with one agency, you
> tie up less of your management and administrative time.

Compare the simplicity of an integrated marketing relationship with the traditional structures of client, agencies and
specialist suppliers. In a large consumer goods company, for
example, you might find brand managers working with different advertising agencies; a marketing director working with
another agency on corporate campaigns; incentives and promotion specialists using their own groups of suppliers. There
could be a publication manager dealing with designers, writers, photographers, new media companies and printers to
produce product literature and point-of-sale; training managers producing and marketing information for the salesforce;
national account managers producing programmes for individual retail outlets. To add to the complexity, there may
also be public relations executives handling press and public
relations activities through a consultancy; a design manager developing a new corporate identity; and a direct mail
specialist to produce consumer direct marketing campaigns.

Each department or individual will be selecting and monitoring suppliers operating to their own standards, raising
purchase orders, checking invoices and creating payment
authorisation. This is time-consuming and inefficient. It
takes up a great deal of management time and it can lead to
duplication of costs and effort.

In integrated marketing, single agencies are appointed
to handle and coordinate all marketing and communication
activities. While they may not handle every type of work
with their own resources, they provide a management service to deal with specialist suppliers – selecting them, briefing
them, evaluating their work and handling all administration
on behalf of the client.

Reduce your marketing costs

Integrated marketing can also save money. Apart from the reduction in administrative costs, consolidating all expenditure in a single agency should mean greater value for money. Key savings might include:

◆ better media rates through centralised buying

◆ rationalisation of product literature

◆ elimination of duplication in areas such as photography

◆ reduction in hidden internal administration costs

◆ competitive centralised buying across all marketing activities.

The benefits of centralised media buying through media independents and full service agencies are well established. Integrated marketing takes it a stage further and ensures that all media are purchased centrally, so the client gets the benefit not only of efficient press, television and radio buying, but also benefits from volume buying of print, artwork and other specialist marketing services. Integrated marketing agencies are able to select the most efficient, cost-effective suppliers and work in long-term partnership with them. Partnership and continuity of work mean that the agency's suppliers can afford to offer more competitive prices and better value for money.

Many integrated marketing agencies utilise international quality standards to manage the quality of their suppliers and their internal processes. This not only improves quality, it can also help to reduce the cost of waste, and that can represent a significant saving.

Integrated marketing reduces a great deal of duplication in the creative and production processes. To take a simple example, photography can be planned in advance to ensure maximum utilisation of location and material. In the case of a car manufacturer, for example, photography would be required for press and television advertisements, videos, product literature, direct mail, point-of-sale, training material and distributor support programmes. If each of these specialist departments or agencies organised its own photography, there would be an enormous element of wastage, not to mention creative disparity.

Integrated marketing ensures that creative resources like this can be utilised in the most cost-effective way. The development of creative treatment could yield further cost savings; as the first part of this chapter demonstrated, creative integrity is a key element of integrated marketing. This means that creative themes are developed centrally and then fine-tuned to the specific needs of each medium. Depending on the method of agency remuneration, this can represent a significant saving on production costs over a complete campaign and reduce the potential duplication of work.

creative resources can be utilised in the most cost-effective way

Integrated marketing in action

To see how integrated marketing works, here's a fictitious campaign designed to broaden the market for a hi-fi system.

The aim of the campaign

The manufacturer has an established reputation for quality hi-fi systems and holds a strong market share in a high price sector. However, the manufacturer is aware that low price competitors are opening up a wider market by making hi-fi more accessible and more affordable for consumers who might have considered only a basic audio system in the past. The manufacturer wants to protect share and margins in the traditional market, but also take advantage of the broader opportunities.

The strategy is to use the established reputation to brand the lower price range, and also demystify hi-fi for the new generation of buyers. The new product range will be marketed initially through popular electrical retailers, leaving the established brands with traditional dealers. However, in the long term, the manufacturer aims to market the whole range through traditional dealers to encourage consumers to trade up to higher price products.

An integrated marketing plan is devised as follows.

Press advertising

National press advertising highlights the affordable hi-fi concept and stresses the brand heritage to reassure consumers that they will have a quality product. Consumers are invited to visit a website or call a freephone number to request a brochure and get the name of their nearest retailer.

Web marketing

Consumers who visit the website are able to download general information about hi-fi, product information and details of retailers. The website includes a page that allows consumers to enter their own hi-fi preferences and build their own system. This helps to demystify hi-fi and also provides the company with valuable information on customer preferences.

Direct marketing follow-up

Respondents are mailed with the offer of taking part in a free prize draw to win a collection of compact discs, whether they buy a system or not. As part of the data-capture process, prospects are asked to provide details of their current audio systems and musical tastes. Future mailings can be highly targeted with offers of music or event promotions that reflect the consumers' tastes.

Retail sales development

To ensure that prospects get the right level of service when they visit a retail outlet, the campaign provides product training for retail staff. The training covers the main features and benefits of hi-fi systems, and tells sales staff how to explain them in non-technical terms that will not intimidate a prospect who just wants to listen to music. To encourage sales staff to sell the product, an incentive programme will operate, offering 20 successful staff the reward of a trip to a great musical location such as Vienna, New York or Sydney.

Retail support

Retailers are provided with point-of-sale material that reflects the consumer advertising themes of affordable hi-fi. Brochures on making the most of hi-fi are available and a free CD offer runs for selected periods. Retailers also have access to a central telemarketing service which can be used to follow up respondents to the initial advertising campaign. Participating retailers can run competitions offering prospects the chance to win free concert tickets if they request a demonstration of the hi-fi system.

Customer information

To maintain the theme of accessible hi-fi, customers receive instructions and product guides in a simple, easy-to-use form. The guides use only non-technical terms and are designed to ensure that customers are fully satisfied with their systems. A 24-hour helpline is available to any customer who needs advice.

Campaign summary

The campaign ensures that hi-fi is presented as a straightforward accessible product from the outset. The manufacturer thus ensures that prospects will not be 'blinded by science' at the retail outlet, and provides help and guidance after the sale.

From integration to joined-up marketing

Many agencies are great advocates of integrated marketing. The logic is simple: encourage interest through broadcast communications then follow through with well-orchestrated direct activity to generate leads for the business to pursue. But this strategy is very much a straightforward consumer-oriented model. For complex business-to-business markets, the customer isn't a single decision maker and the sales process isn't always rapid.

It's at this point that integration is not enough. The campaign proposition has to penetrate far deeper within the business, beyond generating a lead. This places a fundamentally different emphasis on the role of the marketing function and their agency. It's no longer enough to base campaign success on the volume of leads. What's critical is the conversion ratio and quality factor of business wins.

*it's at this point
that integration is
not enough*

> ### Marketing secret
>
> ◆ Marketing activity needs to go beyond stimulating interest – it has to play a crucial part in all stages of the process up until closure. This is where joined-up marketing differs from integrated marketing.

Joined-up marketing places a far greater emphasis on the whole sales process, ensuring that all parties use the core creative messages in a relevant, as well as consistent manner. Each member of the target audience is exposed to a consistent message, but the emphasis changes depending on their views and concerns, objectives and interests. The process of moving to a successful sale requires a communications programme that successfully and successively builds relationships before, during and after the sale, qualifying the process all the way through. Joined-up marketing looks at these requirements and goes beyond simply delivering integrated communications.

> ## Marketing secret
>
> ◆ The process of moving to a successful sale requires a communications programme that successfully and successively builds relationships before, during and after the sale, qualifying the process all the way through.

The goal is to ensure that, at every contact point, communications encourage the decision-making chain to talk among themselves. It isn't about a single communication directed to a specific person. The aim is to encourage people to talk with other people in the organisation. Each person will have their own agenda so they need to be exposed to the right messages about your product or service at the right moment. Some will want financial accountability, others will be concentrating on service levels or how what you offer enhances their own marketing opportunities. The key is to apply the basic message to different decision makers and influencers and, where necessary, refine the proposition to ensure that you aren't simply repeating a message, but building a progressive understanding of the real benefits of your product or service.

Joined-up marketing recognises that in many business sectors, there is a collaborative decision-making process. Joined-up marketing checks that there are no weak links in the communications programme where the message is not reaching the right decision maker. Every point of contact through the course of the sale is an opportunity to reinforce what you stand for, what you deliver and how you differentiate yourself from competitors.

Talk with a single voice

If your customers and prospects are getting the same message from every advertisement, direct mail shot and web page, the impact builds and builds. Consistent messaging reinforces your core brand values and makes your company and your products immediately recognisable. That's why integrated marketing and joined-up marketing bring major benefits of creative consistency, operational efficiency and cost reduction. By speaking with a single voice, your budgets and your campaigns work much harder.

As we'll see in the next chapter, it isn't just the marketing tools that need to be consistent. When everyone in your company is giving customers the same message, the results can be dramatic.

PART 4

People matter: the inside track to success

It's people who make marketing work. Whether you're a member of the marketing team or the person running the show, you depend on many people, both inside and outside the marketing department. This section looks at ways to get more from the people, resources and budgets available to you.

13 Get everyone on board

Your colleagues can be your greatest ambassadors, but only if they know your products, understand your marketplace and are aware of your marketing campaigns. Put internal communications on your priority list and thus add a free promotional tool to your marketing weapons.

14 Expand your team without hiring

If you've got a small marketing team, what do you do when you have to organise a major exhibition or tackle a time-consuming project like a new website? It may be impractical to hire additional staff and existing staff may not have the right skills. Marketing resourcing services are available from specialist recruitment consultancies who supply staff with appropriate skills for the duration of a specific project, completing the project effectively and leaving your team to deal with day-to-day tasks.

15 Partnership – more power to your marketing elbow

Collaboration with business partners can give you access to new products, new technologies, new skills, new markets. Why waste valuable investment funds when a partner can give you immediate access to the resources you need to accelerate marketing success?

16 Measure for measure – just what is marketing success?

Marketing success can be measured in many different ways, but it's important to present your results in terms of return on investment because that is the language financial controllers and board members speak.

13

Get everyone on board

TO SUCCEED IN MARKETING, you depend on many other factors ... and many other people. So just who has the biggest impact on customer satisfaction in your company? Although the marketing, sales and customer service teams are in the front line when it comes to dealing with customers, many other people in your company could be influencing customer satisfaction. Your colleagues in other departments can be your greatest ambassadors, but only if they know your products, understand your marketplace and are aware of your marketing campaigns. Bring them on board and thus add a free promotional tool to your marketing weapons.

The place to start is the sales department. They need to be on your side, because otherwise you could struggle. In many companies there's a lingering perception of a 'gap' between sales and marketing. As a simple example, it's not unusual for salespeople to be promoting products that marketing did not plan to support in the long run, and failing to adequately promote products that marketing do plan to support.

You've probably heard the arguments that go on in the bar after a sales and marketing conference. The sales department makes a real commercial impact because it delivers revenue. Marketing is 'fluffy', only responsible for events and campaigns that take money rather than make it. Such attitudes can lead to a culture of blame between sales and marketing. With the current emphasis on survival, marketing is in danger of losing respect within the company, particularly in comparison with the sales team, who are usually perceived as being directly responsible for making money. If you want to make an impact in your company, you need to close that gap and get the salespeople on your side.

Marketing secret

◆ Eliminating the gap between marketing and sales is key to long-term marketing success.

When you take a closer look at the claims of both sides, you'll find that this blame culture is at its most extreme in the gap between lead generation and closure. In many companies, the marketing process has traditionally stopped at lead generation. The lead then moves to the sales team and the result is that sales and marketing are often acting as two separate organisations with closure rates that can leave considerable room for improvement.

'Marketing generates leads, sales has the responsibility for closing them', so the argument goes. However, industry estimates suggest that around 70 per cent of leads provided are never pursued. The sales department typically believes either that the quality of the lead is poor or that the buyer is not yet ready to make a purchase. And, when closure rates are low, both sides are quick to blame each other. 'The leads are poor quality,' say the sales team. 'The sales team can't close deals,' say the marketing department. Does this sound familiar? If it does, how do you close the gap?

Close the gap

In the worst cases, both parties can take up entrenched positions. Okay, creative marketing activities raise awareness and get the company noticed, but is that enough? Your real aim is to build profitable long-term business, and that's where marketing has traditionally failed to make a real impact. This has become even more critical in the current turbulent economic climate, and you now need to demonstrate commercial awareness and impact throughout the purchase cycle. That means you're going to be involved with the sales team at every stage of the cycle and collaboration is key to closing the gap.

Marketing secret

◆ Working with the sales team at every stage of the purchase cycle is the only way to close the 'gap' between sales and marketing.

For companies in the technology sector, this integrated approach is critical. Here the decision-making process is becoming more and more complex, and the sales/marketing model has to match. A global networking company found that in a typical scenario there may be 6–9 key influencers and a purchase cycle that could last 12–18 months. Generating sales leads through an advertising or direct marketing campaign was just the start. The challenge was to maintain communications with all the key contacts throughout the purchase cycle and move them towards the right buying decision.

For both teams, that meant moving away from a simple model of prospect, qualify, present and close, to a more integrated process in which sales and marketing collaborated, focusing on all the influencers and decision makers in a target company. In this collaborative model, marketing was able to make a bigger impact on sales success by matching marketing communications to the time that was best for the sales process, rather than for the marketing process. That gave the marketing department a greater stakeholding interest in target revenues and closed customers, enhancing its visibility and accountability in terms of return on marketing investment.

Through collaboration, the marketing team acquired a 360-degree view of the purchasing cycle. It also gained a better understanding of sales dynamics and customer relationships. By reducing the gulf between sales and marketing and creating a greater commercial impact, the marketing team helped to build credibility and trust. And, by demonstrating the link between revenue stream and demand creation, they were able to operate at a more strategic level within the company. Rather than the traditional roles of 'fee earners versus enablers', the emphasis for both sales and marketing teams was on profitable business development as a long-term revenue generator.

Marketing secret

◆ Effective collaboration between marketing and sales can create exceptional results.

Beyond lead generation

The clear message from the case above is that, in the context of sales revenue, your job doesn't stop at lead generation. If you want to deliver exceptional results, you've got to build collaboration with *your job doesn't stop* the sales team so that you can reduce the *at lead generation* purchase cycle.

One of the most important ways to do this is through the transfer of leads from marketing to sales. But, as we explained earlier, estimates suggest that currently around 70 per cent of leads provided are never pursued. So, consider putting a mechanism in place to assess the value of leads objectively by assigning a certain weighting to each lead. This approach enables you to prioritise and pass the right opportunities to the most appropriate sales team member as quickly as possible. If your salesforce is focused on priority leads, they are more likely to be successful in closing a sale.

Marketing secret

◆ Sharing prospect intelligence can help sales and marketing teams focus on the prospects with the strongest propensity to buy.

To improve collaboration even further, encourage the salesforce to provide constructive feedback on the reasons why they reject any leads provided by you. It could be, for example, that a sales representative does not deal with a particular industry sector. In that situation, rather than having the lead fall into the gap, it can now be picked up and rerouted to the correct person. Equally, the lead could be strong but the timing poor. Perhaps the prospect is at an early stage in the buying cycle. If so, rather than losing the opportunity, the system can store the lead and you can concentrate on learning more about these leads through communication and feedback. By building trust and interest over time, you will be able to move these prospects through the sales cycle until they are ready to re-engage with the sales team. Typically, it may take two, three or even more contacts before a prospect is ready to engage with sales. Each of these interactions can provide invaluable insight into customer behaviour.

More interaction with prospects is the message and the way to do that is to gather intelligence through a planned research, education and interactive communication process, then use the data to improve the results of your customer acquisition programmes. This approach complements and supports traditional sales activities by prioritising opportunities, maintaining the momentum of customer acquisition and accelerating the purchase process. Here you and the sales team play a larger role in educating, building relationships, and maintaining contact with prospects rather than just focusing on sales closure.

The process is known as prospect relationship management, or lead incubation, and it offers some great benefits. The intelligence gathering and customer feedback can lead to higher sales conversions by helping your sales team to engage continuously with decision makers throughout the acquisition process. What's more, the feedback can be used to fine-tune communications and make them more relevant and engaging with highly-targeted messages.

Keep gathering intelligence

Changing roles, responsibilities and priorities within a decision-making group can impact on the success of a sales and marketing programme, so it is essential to maintain detailed insight into the key targets. Intelligence gathering can help you and the sales team *maintain detailed* improve your understanding of objections *insight into the* and sales hurdles, get better up-to-date *key targets* insight into the role of influencers and decision makers, and build clearer sales profiles as a basis for focusing sales effort on the most appropriate prospects.

This requires an intelligence plan that gathers and builds essential insight throughout the sales and marketing process. One way to gain this continuous insight is through a programme of activities designed to provide useful feedback. We saw earlier in the book how communities can provide valuable feedback – that's great fuel to support the collaborative sales and marketing process. By providing communities of customers and prospects with resources such as white papers and encouraging feedback, you and the sales teams can raise your company's visibility as well as gaining insight into decision making and attitudes.

Marketing secret

◆ Communications that encourage feedback give you insight into a prospect's propensity to buy.

The feedback also enables you to develop relevant value propositions for different members of the decision-making group, based on their responses to the different marketing activities. Here's an example. A white paper emailed to a prospect company was forwarded by the original recipient to different people within the company and created a major discussion topic on the website. The white paper triggered a 'community' that gave valuable insight and helped to support a highly-targeted approach to sales and marketing planning based on a deeper knowledge of the roles and importance of influencing and decision-making groups.

Using intelligence like this to fine-tune communications can also help you personalise messages for each key prospect. By using media that encourage feedback, you can also identify a prospect's propensity to buy at different stages of the campaign. Communications can then be modified, with messaging refocused to reflect individual interests and concerns. You can develop this approach in a number of different 'interactive' media, including:

◆ direct marketing that encourages response

◆ web pages that allow data to be captured

◆ surveys

◆ workshops, white papers, executive briefings and
roundtables

◆ web-based communities.

Time for new job descriptions?

As sales and marketing collaboration grows, a shift in the job
market has been generated, with recruitment consultancies
reporting some significant changes in job responsibilities
among sales and marketing staff. Commercial awareness is
now a definite consideration when companies recruit marketing staff and this changing perspective is reflected in the
relative importance of different job descriptions. Job titles
like 'field marketing' have been around for a
while but, until recently, they have not been   *be closer to where the*
particularly visible within the marketing   *selling happens*
department. Terms like 'sales enablement'
and 'customer relationship management' are appearing
more frequently in marketing recruitment advertisements.
Emerging responsibilities like this are an indication that,
today, you and your colleagues in marketing have to be
closer to where the selling happens.

Marketing secret

◆ Recruit staff who can bridge the gap between marketing
and sales.

Although traditional job titles such as 'marketing manager' are still widely used, your responsibilities must continue to develop, bringing marketing, revenue, business development and measurement functions under one roof. You now have a much greater responsibility for their contribution to the bottom line because companies buy in to the results, as opposed to the product or process of how to get the end result. With the current economic climate, you have to be much more 'business ready'. In short, you have to represent a truly quantifiable benefit to your company.

Focus on all customer-facing staff

Collaboration with the sales team is crucial to marketing success, but it's important not to overlook the contribution that other departments can also make. Before your company can deliver the standards of service that build and maintain the highest levels of customer satisfaction, you must ensure that everyone in the company is committed to customer care and understands their role in it.

It's not just the people who deliver the service, you need buy-in from the executive team to ensure commitment from the top and the right level of resources committed to the project. And you have to persuade departmental managers to encourage their staff to offer the highest standards of service. In some cases, they will have to change their priorities to build the right standards of service. They may need to change their working practices or to send some of their staff on training courses so that they achieve the right standards. You first need to convince them that this is as important as meeting their day-to-day business objectives.

The front-line service staff who are in regular contact with customers may need more detailed information on the actions they are to take and their changing role in a partnership situation. Some of them will already be aware of their contribution to customer satisfaction, but others, as we'll see later, may take some convincing.

Communicating with customer-facing staff is vital to the success of any external marketing initiative. Strong customer relationships are a critical issue because of the high cost of finding and winning new customers, in comparison to serving existing customers. An investment in communications with customer-facing staff is therefore a cost-effective strategy. These employees are in direct contact with customers in a variety of different ways – face-to-face, online, or on the telephone. Customer relationships depend on the attitude, knowledge and loyalty of this group. If they are committed and fully-informed 'champions' they can make a major contribution to building long-term customer loyalty.

> *Marketing secret*
> ◆ Staff who are fully informed become 'champions' who make a major contribution to building long-term customer loyalty.

Empower the hidden communicators

Sometimes, it may not be obvious who to involve – some staff who are not directly in touch with customers and who may be overlooked in a customer care training programme

take a look around your company might still have an impact on customer service. Take a look around your company at the likely candidates – they might include accounts clerks who produce inaccurate invoices, warehouse staff who pick the wrong parts, or departmental managers who refuse to cooperate in allocating resources to customer-facing activities.

Marketing secret

◆ Some of the people who impact customer satisfaction may never come into direct contact with a customer. Internal marketing makes them aware of their role and responsibilities.

In many businesses, it is the people who deliver the service – the technicians and engineers – who are crucial. However, they may be 'hidden away', never exposed to a customer. Any customer complaints are filtered, and the customer never gets an opportunity to talk directly with the people responsible for the problems. It is the barriers between the customer and the people who provide the service that make internal marketing programmes so important.

A manufacturing company once ran a programme called 'Put yourself in their shoes', aimed at those 'hidden' members of the team. The programme described the impact poor service had on customers by describing a series of incidents that resulted from mistakes and oversights by different departments. The programme highlighted areas for improvement and, more importantly, demonstrated to the departments that they had an important role to play in customer satisfaction. By the end of the programme, customer satisfaction levels had risen significantly while the costs of remedial action fell, giving a good return on the programme investment.

When trying to identify the 'hidden persuaders', it's important to remember that internal customers do not represent a single homogenous market. Like external customers, different groups will have their own behaviour and different levels of awareness. One recommended form of segmentation is to divide employees into three groups:

1 Supporters.

2 Neutral.

3 Opponents.

Each group requires a slightly different internal marketing mix to ensure that you achieve your internal marketing objectives. For example, if you wanted to introduce changes in the way that your customer service team dealt with customers, you could target the supporters with communications explaining how to implement the changes. You could encourage the neutrals to participate with an incentive programme linked to service training and you could target the opponents with more persuasive forms of communication designed to change attitudes.

Marketing secret

◆ Make sure your internal marketing programme targets 'opponents' as well as 'supporters'.

Talk to customers with a single voice

Internal marketing empowers your staff to build stronger customer relationships through greater involvement, commitment and understanding. It's also a way of ensuring you deliver consistent messages to your customers. Handle field sales, advertising, direct marketing, customer service, and telesales through different departments or external agencies and your customers could be receiving a different message every time they contact you. That 'diversity' could be costing you money as well. You may be missing additional sales opportunities, and you could be duplicating some of your customer management costs.

Talking to customers with a single voice ensures high-impact marketing campaigns, increases retention rates and maximises return on marketing investments. Internal marketing should therefore feature the same messages that you use in external communications. There's an added bonus – when employees understand and commit to your company's value proposition and brands, external marketing becomes more effective because the employees become product champions.

By adopting a positive internal marketing programme, you can add many more people to your marketing resources, turning them into well-informed ambassadors for the company, your brands and your products. And, there's an added bonus – when you've got your colleagues on board, you'll find it easier to encourage innovation throughout the company.

Create a culture of innovation

Innovation is critical for companies who want to remain competitive in the long term. It's a key discipline within product development and it underpins quality customer service. Although many companies recognise its importance, it can be difficult to identify the sources of innovation and create an innovative culture. Although innovation is likely to originate within a product development group, the most productive solution is to build a culture where people throughout the company are proactive in developing innovative ideas.

It's important to distinguish between innovation and invention. Invention is the process of discovering things that have never been discovered before. In business, innovation is the discovery of new ways of creating value. To achieve that, employees don't have to be working in product development or a research team. Their day-to-day experiences of working with customers or overcoming challenges can highlight better ways of dealing with an issue. So, although few people are likely to be inventors, anyone can be innovative.

Marketing secret
- ◆ Small ideas can make a major contribution to customer satisfaction.

An important element in building company-wide innovation is to encourage small improvements, rather than looking for the 'big idea'. For example, you could ask employees to look at different aspects of the business. How can the company improve delivery to customers, save money on office supplies or promote products in a different way? The ideas can be very simple and probably only a few will be useful. Nonetheless, this approach encourages people to contribute.

The challenge is to build a culture that encourages all employees to contribute to innovation. This can be difficult when employees and managers are focused on day-to-day pressures or when departments are used to working in isolation.

> ### Marketing secret
>
> ◆ Building an innovation community spreads the load and spreads the word.

A manufacturing company recognised this problem and decided to move forward by progressing in stages. First, it put together a team of people who could drive innovation. This team was responsible for raising awareness of innovation, building any necessary infrastructure, creating the training materials and plans, and developing a process for managing innovation. The team included people from all departments, particularly customer-facing departments, and marketing was at its core. The aim was to ensure that all departments recognised their responsibilities and opportunities. The company recognised that a specialist team was an essential first stage, but that

innovation should be the responsibility of everyone in the company

it should be seen only as a starting point. After a period of time, innovation should be the responsibility of everyone in the company, not just a specialist group.

They soon found that members of the innovation team were taking on different roles and responsibilities, depending on their experience and attitudes. People regarded as true innovators tended to do things differently, breaking the rules and ignoring traditional ways of doing things. More conservative team members were prepared to adapt and make improvements, but worked within the rules and accepted the status quo. The group also included people who were good at detailed planning and others who lacked planning skills but were good at implementing solutions and making things work.

If you're planning to spread the word on innovation, try to get a balance of these characteristics.

Build an innovation community

An effective team can achieve great results, but one of its most important roles is to spread the load and build a commitment to innovation throughout a company. For the manufacturing company described above, the next stage was to create an 'innovation community' – a larger group that represented the specific needs of departments, as well as championing the needs of customers, business partners and other stakeholders. The community operated informally, but built relations with the innovation team, identifying needs and communicating those needs to the team. Community members carried out a range of important tasks to support the company's innovation drive. One group delivered workshops to explain and encourage innovation within different departments. Another stimulated innovative ideas through describing best practice and running brainstorming sessions. And, to capture the benefit of those sessions, they prepared case studies which proved invaluable for later projects.

If you're aiming to create this kind of environment, it's important to provide facilities to support the innovation community. You can set up a 'virtual community' on the Internet or your company intranet to support communications and collaborative working between people with a common interest. Facilities to support the community could include newsletters, discussion groups and information. An online discussion group gives users the facilities for posting messages on the innovation community site. The messages should represent helpful information and may include requests for help or further information. Some sites set up facilities for feedback or review, introducing an opportunity for objective, independent comment. The aim is to encourage other members of the community to suggest answers, provide help or contribute to the discussion of a specific issue. Discussion groups help to strengthen the relationships that are essential to a company-wide culture of innovation.

If the community is successful, they can spread understanding and commitment to innovation throughout the company. The objective is to make innovation an everyday activity. By this stage the responsibility for change and innovation no longer rests with an individual.

the objective is to make innovation an everyday activity

Employees take over responsibility themselves and see innovation as an essential part of their jobs. You can encourage good contributions by recognising and highlighting the ideas that get accepted. Put the best ideas onto the innovation website and involve other employees. The key is a commitment from top management to implement the best ideas. If your employees have the prospect of their ideas being accepted and rewarded, they will contribute.

All aboard

It's clear from the above examples that marketing works best when it involves everyone in a company. Your natural partners are the salesforce, but working in the background are all those people whose jobs bring them into direct or indirect contact with customers. Encourage them, involve them and keep them informed on what the company is doing and where it's going. When people make a positive contribution to success, recognise their achievement and reward it. It may not be marketing in the conventional sense, but it will certainly add a valuable resource and edge to your efforts.

As we'll see in the next chapter, expanding your team without hiring is also a great way to improve marketing performance.

14

Expand your team without hiring

NO MATTER HOW GREAT a team you have, sometimes you need skills and resources that are simply not available from your current people. Short-term marketing programmes such as exhibitions or events can impose considerable pressure on the existing team, distracting them from their main priorities, and sometimes leading to demoralisation and poor results.

One solution would be retraining, but that takes time and deadlines are often be tight. You could also consider recruiting full-time staff with specialist skills to manage projects such as roadshows or website development. But, if these projects are only short-term, you may find that the specialists are under-used and this could prove an expensive solution. So, which way do you go? You need to make the project a success, but you don't need the fixed costs of permanent staff, particularly when you have to take into consideration the full cost of recruiting, training and employing them.

Resourcing

In such situations, smart companies have turned to a recruitment process called resourcing – hiring specialists for the period of a specific project – and it has proved a flexible alternative to retraining or permanent recruitment of new staff. These companies have found that resourcing is ideal for acquiring specialist skills on a short- or mid-term basis for projects such as events, conferences, product launches or other tactical campaigns. It also provides a cost-effective solution to those inevitable peaks and troughs in marketing activity.

What's new about resourcing?

Hiring contract staff has been around for a long time, so you could reasonably ask, 'What's new about resourcing?' Isn't it just a new term for an existing service? There's a difference. If you do take on contract staff in the traditional way, you're normally required to hire them for a fixed period – 3 months, 6 months or a year, for example. Resourcing is a more flexible option, giving you the option of taking on the skills you need for short or long periods, depending on the project duration.

resourcing is a more flexible option

The other major difference is that the resourcing specialists work directly for a recruitment agency, but are based in your marketing department as an integral part of your team. To create that 'team member' feeling, agencies aim to recruit resourcing candidates with the confidence to adapt to multi-skilled roles in a marketing environment. They also look for people who are good at building relationships with other professionals so that they can contribute effectively to your marketing team. Instead of relative 'outsiders', you have focused team players with the drive and expertise to turn opportunities into profitable results.

> *Marketing secret*
> ◆ Resourcing staff are focused on results, not office politics.

Resourcing can take you further

You might think that it's only appropriate to hire resourcing staff to fill a gap or provide temporary cover for team members who are on leave. That's a legitimate and widely-practised role for contracting, but resourcing goes much further. The resourcing approach is much more focused on results – the emphasis is on delivery. That focus works both ways, because it gives the resourcing members a greater sense of involvement in the work and success of your team.

the emphasis is on delivery

Experience indicates that resourcing staff can bring commitment, energy and enthusiasm to a marketing department. They are good team players and would be able to work effectively with other members of your team to enable you to meet your goals. One small but important advantage they have is that they are outside the politics that go with being permanent staff. They are able to focus their efforts on getting the job done rather than getting embroiled in office politics or team bureaucracy.

There is a perception that no external specialist could match the accumulated in-house skills, knowledge and experience of your own marketing team. While that may be true, just how essential is that? The reality is that your marketing department can use resourcing to acquire specific marketing expertise without adding headcount. So, resourcing adds to the capability and experience within a team and complements it.

The type of people who go into resourcing have the market insight to bring a depth of understanding of the decision-making processes and key challenges you

they bring strategic vision and an ability to work effectively

face. They can work effectively with other members of your team and identify the marketing programmes that will enable you to meet your goals. To enhance your business development programmes and achieve an effective return on marketing investment, they bring strategic vision and an ability to work effectively with your sales, marketing and product development teams. They apply acquired industry knowledge and experience of what works well, and what doesn't, from previous employment. This allows them to hit the ground running and help you achieve results in essential areas.

Make better use of your staff budget

There's a popular belief that resourcing is expensive and that it's cheaper to keep everything including skills and project delivery in-house. In reality, this is probably a short-sighted view, particularly if you look at the bigger picture. By taking on resourcing staff for those special projects, your department can acquire skills, services and flexibility without the hassle of overheads, sick pay, redundancy payouts and other recurring employment costs. What's more, hiring is time-consuming work and recruitment agencies aren't cheap, although they do take a lot of the pain out of the process. Given the 'total cost of ownership' of employees, you would need a strong case for recruiting permanent staff for specific projects. The *the savings can be* resourcing model removes 'people costs' *significant* such as pension and private health contributions, as well as training, recruitment, human resources management, payroll and social costs from the equation. The savings can be significant, particularly when typical recruitment agency fees of 20 per cent are taken into account.

While it's true that some specialists are in constant demand because of their outstanding skills, and earn substantially more than internal staff, the overall cost of hiring in project-based resourcing staff is likely to be competitive with internal team costs. And there's another potential advantage. The cost of resourcing staff can be charged to a separate services budget, removing it from fixed overheads. That improves financial flexibility, particularly when there is pressure to reduce departmental budgets.

Marketing secret

◆ If you haven't got a budget for additional permanent staff, consider hiring contract staff using a services budget.

One example is a telecommunications company that was aiming to cut its costs by reducing headcount across all departments. The marketing department faced the prospect of losing two experienced executives who would be essential in meeting their targets over the coming year. Their solution was to make the executives redundant, which met their internal requirements. The executives then joined a resourcing agency who hired them back to the company with payment from a marketing services budget. The company was able to show reduced overheads, but was able to maintain the momentum of its essential marketing programmes.

Build a more responsive marketing environment

If you need to create a more responsive marketing environment to adapt to changing market conditions, accelerate rollout of strategic programmes or improve return on marketing investment, you'll find that traditional marketing structures may prove inadequate.

You need to look more closely at the efficiency and costs of recruiting, managing and supporting a fully-staffed marketing department. Resourcing offers a highly-efficient, cost-effective alternative model that offers important business benefits while reducing costs, improving response to market opportunities, accelerating programme deployment and maintaining marketing momentum. Companies who have implemented resourcing report a number of important benefits, including:

- reduction in programme deployment times
- quicker response to market opportunities
- savings on consolidated marketing service costs
- more dynamic, flexible marketing team
- more effective solution than recruitment or stretching existing resources
- enhanced team performance by providing diverse or specialist skills on a short- or mid-term basis
- cost-effective solution to peaks and troughs in marketing activity.

Where to use resourcing

With so many potential benefits, where can you use resourcing?

Marketing secret

- Specialist tasks require specialist skills. With resourcing you can bring in the skills you need on a project by project basis.

Support marketing communications

A company with its own internal advertising department found that it was unable to cope with the changing pattern of communications. The team were experienced in press and television, but didn't have the skills to handle online campaigns or e-marketing. Pressure on budgets and a demand for better return on marketing investment meant that they had to deliver results and demonstrate that they were adding value across all media. Resourcing provided the back-up they needed for their long-term assignment of developing an online presence and for a series of critical email campaigns.

Support events

Events are a key element in many industry sectors, contributing to the success of product and service launches, partner activities and product communications. However, they can also represent a drain on budgets and resources, as one automotive manufacturer found, so they must be highly focused with tangible and demonstrable benefits. The company had committed to run a series of local dealership events which were proving to be time-limited, but resource-intensive. The marketing department was struggling to give the events the time and commitment they needed. A resourcing agency provided them with an event specialist who delivered the right mix of organisational, logistics and planning skills to manage the programme over a 9-month period. The events helped to drive traffic to the dealerships and contributed to revenue, without tying up the marketing department's own resources.

Support markets and sectors

Focusing on a specific sector or regional market significantly improves your marketing precision and return on investment. It's vital to fully understand the current issues and challenges for individual niche markets, whether you segment them by horizontal or vertical sector, size of business or region. This tight focus means you don't just communicate the relevant benefits and value points of your products, you also deliver them in a way that recognises the concerns of key decision makers in each sector. However, as a technology company realised, it can be difficult to find that detailed sector knowledge in a team with general marketing skills. The company wanted to establish leadership in a number of different sectors, with a particular emphasis on the public sector. Through a resourcing agency, they were able to bring in a marketing executive with experience in that sector. Over a six-month period, the executive built up effective liaison with many different internal departments, transferring his own sector knowledge. With valuable client contacts in the sector, the executive was also able to add value to the company's lead generation campaigns.

Support channels

Developing indirect channels is becoming increasingly critical to competitiveness and profitability. It's vital to identify and build the right relationships, maximise opportunities and improve performance. An insurance company that had previously built its business on direct sales over the Internet, realised that future growth would depend on building productive relationships with brokers and other potential partners. Through resourcing, they were able to bring in a financial services specialist with a combination of marketing, business development and strategic skills. The executive developed a series of programmes to recruit brokers and, at the same time, set up a channel marketing team to maintain relationships with the brokers and give the indirect channel the attention it needed.

Support alliances and partnerships

Increasingly, companies are looking towards alliance relationships as the route to strategic growth and enhanced competitiveness. However, many businesses do not have the resources to establish and manage a strategic alliance. A telecommunications company that wanted to move into new markets recognised that it would need to work with partners to source the technology and services needed to succeed. It used resourcing to bring in a professional with the skills and experience to manage the alliances and partner development activities. The executive set up an alliance infrastructure and took responsibility for the initial execution and management of co-market development activities. As a result, the company was able to attract partners who were leaders in their field and who recognised that the alliance would prove mutually beneficial.

Support online activities

Companies are putting an increasing emphasis on interactive and online marketing as they seek to squeeze even more value from shrinking budgets. E-marketing offers extremely high levels of precision and cost-effectiveness, while the use of the web to run tactical campaigns and provide customer information has proved to be a fast, convenient medium that outperforms conventional print in terms of cost and flexibility. Given the specialist skills needed to succeed online, many companies use specialist external suppliers, but there may be projects where it's important to have an internal resource. A company marketing seasonal products ran a large-scale e-commerce site that required frequent updating during the peak sales period. The pressure on the external supplier and the problems of liaison had led to some serious problems in previous years, so the company decided to manage the website internally during the crucial period. Through resourcing, they were able to draw on the services of a specialist who maintained an up-to-date dynamic web presence that ensured the company was able to operate an efficient ordering process in line with customer demand and stock availability.

Consider using marketing consultants

While resourcing staff can provide you with the additional project expertise you might need from time to time, what do you do when you need high-level expertise to tackle strategic marketing challenges or the problems of change?

Marketing consultants can support existing marketing programmes, accelerate progress or create new business opportunities by providing expert advice, guidance, counselling, coaching or project management. Consultants bring the experience and capability to turn objectives into plans, action and results. They can bring clarity to difficult decisions through their first-hand experience of the challenges facing growing businesses, especially the need to increase profitability through improved alignment of marketing, sales, brand, and product development activities.

Consultants can also offer advanced skills in applying strategic marketing techniques to successfully steer your business into new territory. They can act as a catalyst to help your company rethink its marketing strategy to meet new opportunities or keep pace with market changes. They can also help your business grow and become more profitable by pursuing new business initiatives to boost growth, perhaps entering new markets, introducing new products, or establishing innovative services.

> *Marketing secret*
>
> ◆ Consultants bring an objective viewpoint that can be valuable when you have to make difficult decisions.

Consultants' independence from internal issues enables them to offer a more objective view. It can also provide a level of authority that can cut through inertia and stimulate productive action. This external perspective can be particularly useful when tackling topics such as branding and messaging, where internal staff may be too close to provide a customer-focused perspective.

Good consultants also transfer knowledge, encouraging your internal team to grow in experience and confidence. They provide a rich source of information and knowledge of

good consultants also transfer knowledge

marketing strategy and programmes that improve internal skills and understanding. Many consultants publish original thought leadership papers, practical advice and references to useful marketing resources, as well as regular news and updates on marketing through newsletters. Consultants' websites often represent a valuable repository of insights and techniques, based on their experience of running marketing programmes and delivering consultancy.

Doing more for less

Hiring consultants or specialists on a resourcing basis can provide your team with the additional skills needed to tackle time-consuming or difficult projects. Resourcing has proved to be a cost-effective solution that can deliver effective results and save money. It meets the needs of many different types of project and gives you the opportunity to move into new markets or focus on projects or activities that have previously been neglected. One key benefit is the transfer of knowledge to the existing team. The specialists may leave at the end of the project, but they leave behind valuable intellectual capital that enables you to build on their work.

This is great for individual projects; but, if your company wants to take on resources on a larger scale, you could consider partnerships or strategic alliances, as the next chapter explains.

15

Partnership – more power to your marketing elbow

COLLABORATION WITH BUSINESS PARTNERS can give your company access to new products, new technologies, new skills and new markets. Why waste valuable investment funds when a partner can give you immediate access to the resources you need to accelerate marketing success? Collaborating on product development programmes, for example, can help you reduce production costs, make better use of skilled, specialist resources and speed up time-to-market. Partnership brings together the objective knowledge, experience and specialist skills of people from different companies who can contribute to the development of your new product more effectively than individual team members in one company performing their own tasks.

Marketing secret
◆ Partnership expands your marketing resources with access to new skills, expertise and business opportunities.

This can be important if you are trying to compete in an increasingly competitive marketplace or moving into new markets. You may be feeling the pressure of a shorter product lifecycle, as customers demand more and more innovative features and benefits. Competitive pressures mean you have to reduce the time and effort involved in bringing products to market. By collaborating and creating efficient joint project teams, you can tackle key challenges in the product development process, improve the success rate of new products, and grow market share and revenue.

Partnership can bring your company a number of important benefits:

◆ Access to scarce skills not available in your own organisation.

◆ Additional resources to tackle larger development projects or reduce lead times.

◆ Access to technologies, components or supplies that can enhance your own product.

◆ Opportunities to enter new markets where the partner has an established presence.

◆ Greater marketing resources.

◆ Access to partners' distribution channels.

Speed up product development

Collaborative product development can help you get a new product to market in the shortest possible time to gain competitive advantage. To achieve this, it's vital that you and your partners integrate all product development activities within a common framework. In collaborative development, the programme can be divided into smaller critical activities which are then handled by appropriate partners. As well as design and manufacturing processes, you can use external partnership services to handle market and customer research, distribution, marketing communications and product launch. By establishing long-term partnerships with specialists, you can reduce the learning period and ensure that every aspect of new product development and launch is handled quickly and efficiently.

integrate all product development activities within a common framework

---

Marketing secret

◆ Partnership can accelerate the pace of innovation by introducing new skills and fresh perspective.

You can also create a stronger culture of innovation by bringing in partners. Many companies are finding that, to maintain the pace of innovation and compete effectively, they need to involve external specialists in this way. Partnership allows your company to focus on its core strengths and introduce expertise, experience and skills that you may not have inside the company. That means including suppliers, partners and customers in an extended enterprise, with the aim of creating higher-quality products through increased innovation and a fresh perspective that can stimulate radical new solutions.

In the pharmaceutical market, partnerships with universities, specialist research laboratories and health organisations enable manufacturers to accelerate their own new product development programmes and ensure that they are at the cutting edge of industry developments. This has encouraged many companies in this sector to locate in areas that are regarded as centres of excellence in medical research, such as Cambridge or Oxford in the UK.

Those external technical skills and resources can also help you increase the level of innovation without investment in your own skills. You could use a partner's technical resources to handle product development on a subcontract basis, gaining access to specialist resources or additional research and development capacity to improve the performance of your own product development programmes. Alternatively, you could use a partner's technical expertise to develop new products that they could not achieve themselves. This provides you with new technology and allows you to diversify in line with their specialist skills.

Offer customers a wider range of products and services

As well as improving your own product development process, you can use a partner's products and services to expand your own portfolio and increase potential revenue and account control. For example, by using a partner's services organisation, you can offer your customers a wide range of after-sales support services without setting up your own infrastructure. This provides new sources of revenue and also increases your control over the customer.

A services organisation that began life as an internal company division, supporting only the company's own products recognised that, to succeed in changing market conditions, it would have to support products from many different companies. It did not have the skills to support other products to the same quality standards as its own products, so it set up alliances with other services organisations. However, to maintain quality standards, the company set a series of service level agreements for partners and backed those with training in customer care. As a result, the services organisation was able to win a much wider variety of contracts and build its reputation in new markets.

Partners' products can fill gaps in your own range or provide products that enable you to enter new market sectors. You can either treat the partner products as 'white label', market them under your own brand or retain the partner name, and draw on the strengths of their marketing. As well as filling in gaps in your own range, you can use partner products to offer customers higher or lower priced versions of your existing products, expanding your market opportunities without compromising your core product values and quality.

Increase your geographical reach

partnership can provide you with a 'shortcut' to local representation

If you are considering expansion into regional markets or international markets, partnership can provide you with a 'shortcut' to local representation. If your partners have a network of local branch offices or distributors, this can provide you with a ready-made infrastructure for providing a local service to your customers. This approach has a number of potential benefits:

◆ Partners' local knowledge and contacts can help you establish your own network.

◆ You can use existing branches to distribute your products.

◆ You have the opportunity to work on a network basis, whereby the partners operate in geographically separate territories but cooperate and share facilities so that each partner can offer its customers a broader service.

A logistics company that wanted to expand its international presence recognised that effective communications would be a vital success factor. The company was able to set up a joint venture with other established logistics companies in a number of territories, but found that the partners' existing communications networks were inadequate. To bring communications up to standard, they formed a further partnership with a global telecommunications company that was able to offer the company access to high-quality networking in all target territories. This gave the company the infrastructure it needed to provide customers with a high quality service, without investing any of its own capital in building new networks.

To assess these opportunities, you need to evaluate the strength and performance of partners' networks:

◆ Can they provide a quality local service to your customers?

◆ Are their existing local networks performing well?

◆ How does their geographical coverage compare with your targets?

◆ Do their performance standards match your requirements?

> *Marketing secret*
>
> ◆ Partnership can allow you to expand geographically without committing your own local resources.

Using partner resources in this way allows you to quickly establish a local presence and test the market before committing further resources to international expansion. It means you can respond quickly to local opportunities and build your international presence step-by-step without compromising existing markets.

Build an effective partnership structure

There are strong, clear marketing benefits in partnerships and this form of collaboration is now common in many industry sectors. You'll find that many companies now list their partnerships and strategic alliances on their website as a demonstration of their extended capability. The most successful partnerships are those that are managed effectively and this has become an important strategic marketing role, with a number of companies appointing specialists to get the greatest benefit from their partners.

the most successful partnerships are those that are managed effectively

Managing partnerships has three key roles:

◆ Setting and managing relationships.

◆ Building and supporting partnership teams.

◆ Managing the communications infrastructure.

Although partners may have strong individual business and marketing objectives, it's essential that any collaborative development project works to a single objective agreed by all the partners. The success of the project could be damaged if each partner insists on following their own development agenda. The result may be a compromise that does not fulfil the new product's full potential. If collaborating companies have an effective working relationship and agree on a single strategy, the result will exceed what they could achieve individually.

Marketing secret

◆ Many companies are appointing specialists to manage the partnership process more effectively.

Support effective teamwork

Effective partnership requires a culture that encourages teamwork, cooperation and collaboration. That means each team member must have clearly defined *collaboration requires* responsibilities within an agreed product *effective teamwork* development process based on sharing of information and collaboration. There are often conflicting goals in product development, so collaboration requires effective teamwork where team members trust and respect one another. There must be open communication and a willingness to accept input from others.

Collaboration has become easier through tools like video-conferencing and the use of secure extranets. Working together in the same location would be an ideal solution, but travel costs could prove prohibitive if the partner companies are far apart. However, secure communication systems and sophisticated collaboration tools mean that dispersed team members can work together effectively in a 'virtual enterprise'. By using collaborative technologies, partnership teams can share accurate, up-to-date digital product information across different companies, as well as across different functions like design, engineering, manufacturing, marketing, sales, and purchasing. Members of the extended team can post suggestions, reviews and other feedback. It's also possible to set up virtual project rooms where teams from different organisations can collaborate on a project using the site database and pull in third-party resources as they need them.

The tools and technologies include:

◆ email to exchange drawings, models and project information

◆ meetings held by teleconferencing and video-conferencing

◆ meetings held via the Internet

◆ project websites to create a single source of project documentation, with email alerts for updates

◆ websites to enable team members to view and comment on project documents or drawings

◆ tools for product data and product information management.

For effective collaborative development, information must be shared more frequently, in a wider variety of ways among dispersed team members. With the right technology solution, you can create an 'open network' that supports communication and collaboration across all the parties involved in a joint product development project. Team members can access knowledge that has typically been trapped in departmental systems, and the collective knowledge allows the team to develop and go to market as one integrated company, rather than as a number of separate isolated groups.

When team members are located in different sites or even different countries, it's essential to ensure that everyone is working with the same up-to-date information. When data is created at multiple sites, it can be difficult to track and maintain an up-to-date history of the communications and decisions relating to the development project. The process can slow down if essential data is missing, out of date, or incorrect. Secure access to current information gives the team confidence that, as changes occur, they're precisely tracked. If all team members are notified immediately when changes to designs or schedules occur, it means fewer development errors, less duplication of effort, and minimal project downtime.

Synchronise launch activities

As well as reducing your product development costs, partnership can also provide financial benefits through joint marketing activities. Effective partnership marketing can make budgets work harder and increase sales when partners work together to provide solutions that meet customers' needs.

A combination of collaborative development and cooperative marketing can deliver an impressive return on investment.

> *Marketing secret*
> ◆ Cooperative marketing can make your budgets go further and ensure successful product launches.

It's essential to agree on a joint creative strategy that communicates effectively with the target audience and does not weaken the proposition through compromise. Joint marketing activities can include:

◆ press releases

◆ information on partners' own websites

◆ joint website

◆ advertising

◆ product guides

◆ white papers

◆ product launch.

Choose the right partners

When you are planning a collaborative project, it's vital to choose the right partners. Your partners should add value to your own offer, or provide other benefits such as access to scarce skills, faster time to market or reduced costs. As well as tangible benefits,

your partners should add value to your own offer

it's important that your partners share your own business and marketing values ... and recognise mutual benefit in working with you.

This checklist can help you assess the potential of a partnership:

◆ commitment to the project

◆ future direction

◆ market experience

◆ technical expertise

◆ management capability

◆ financial stability

◆ quality processes

◆ adequate resources

◆ policy of collaboration.

Track record is a key factor in partnership. Are your partners capable of understanding your requirements and have they already developed successful solutions in your market? They may be the market leader or have a growing market share. Alternatively their market knowledge may be specialised – focused on specific niche markets or sectors which are of interest to you.

Gaining access to a partner's technical expertise is one of the major reasons for forming partnerships. A track record in technical innovation or leadership is one method of demonstrating capability, but partners should also be interested in the potential for future development. Look at potential partners' annual expenditure on research and development, record in new product development, and technical and research resources to substantiate their claims of technical expertise. The quality and experience of their technical staff and their ability to work closely with other technical teams will help the partnership to produce practical results.

Marketing secret

◆ Partnership is a long-term process. Look for partners who are financially stable with the resources to support a growing relationship.

You need to have confidence that your partners can continue to provide you with the same high standards of service over the long term. If there are any doubts about financial stability, you may not wish to commit to a full partnership in which they are the sole supplier. Make sure that you have a full understanding of the financial structure and performance of your partner's organisation. Find out about any major investment programmes that they are carrying out and ask them to provide you with regular information on their financial performance.

Partnership is a long-term commitment and your partners must demonstrate that they have the resources to provide the level of service you need, both now and in the future. What are the key facts about their organisation – size, number of employees, location, turnover and profitability, national or international network? This will help you decide whether they can handle your target level of business. For example, if your customers operate a national or international network of branches, could you use that network to meet your local needs?

Profit from a business ecosystem

If your company has benefited from partnerships or strategic alliances, you could make further gains by becoming a member of a business ecosystem. Business ecosystems are loose networks of customers, manufacturers, suppliers, distributors, service providers, manufacturers of related products or services, technology providers, and other support organisations who rely on the strength of the network as a whole for their own success. Member companies do not depend on their own internal capabilities for success, they can draw on the skills and resources of partners. Members aim to improve the overall health of their ecosystems by contributing to a set of common assets that other companies can use to improve their own competitive performance. This might take the form of communications tools to connect members, or knowledge and resources to speed up and simplify the development of new products by other members.

> *Marketing secret*
> ◆ A business ecosystem provides you with the support of a wide range of partners who can enhance and expand your own customer offering.

Silicon Valley is an example of a business ecosystem. Within the community is the full web of expertise necessary to develop, fund, deliver, market and support an IT solution, including software developers, product integrators, resellers, specialist subcontractors, service providers, investors and specialists in IT sales and marketing. Typically, these are the types of members needed to create a successful ecosystem.

The same principles apply in automotive or aerospace industries for example, where 'clusters' of manufacturers, suppliers and subcontractors are often located in close proximity. This makes collaboration easier and also cuts logistics costs by reducing journey times. These clusters often generate high levels of skills that member companies can draw on and they offer innovative start-up companies the opportunity to build their business quickly. In mid-Essex in the UK, a number of leading electronics companies positively encourage the development of new businesses through an innovation ecosystem that benefits all parties. However, a single geographical location is not essential; collaboration over the Internet means that business ecosystems can be built on global networks spanning several time zones.

Many business ecosystems include members who would normally be considered competitors. However, within the ecosystem, they cooperate to protect and develop the ecosystem – a situation called 'coopetition' – meaning cooperative competition. Members can cooperate in many different ways – defining technical standards, sharing best practices, sponsoring market studies or lobbying government. In the

cooperate to protect and develop the ecosystem

IT sector, for example, firms may jointly agree on technical standards and then develop products that compete with each other using those same standards. By coming together within networks, firms are able to cooperate dynamically and offer complex services, they can create new market opportunities, combine their knowledge, products and services, and jointly produce and offer new services and products.

Smaller companies outside a business ecosystem may have suffered lack of resources, skilled labour, or affordable communications solutions. The new model emphasises networking, knowledge transfer and shared learning. Dynamic networking allows firms to build communities that share business, knowledge, and infrastructures. Business ecosystems offer smaller companies the same possibility that large structured enterprises benefit from, to dynamically aggregate services and organisations, exchanging knowledge, finding partnerships and boosting market demand.

Encourage shared innovation

An important characteristic of business ecosystems is their ability to encourage and support innovation throughout the network. Lead companies help to create value for the rest of the ecosystem in different ways, but the first requirement usually involves the creation of a platform, an asset in the form of services, tools, or technologies that offers solutions to other members. This can take the form of physical assets, like the efficient manufacturing capabilities that larger companies offer to members that don't have their own facilities, or an intellectual asset, like a software platform.

Members of a business ecosystems can leverage their partners' skills and resources for a wide range of business functions, apart from development of core products and business strategy. For example, they can use partners for sales, marketing, manufacturing, technical support and customer training. This provides a flexible, scalable business model that allows companies to rapidly expand or change their operations in line with customer demand using partner resources, rather than slower, longer-term investments. Using partners around the world also enables international expansion without setting up local operations.

One of the ways to improve quality and performance within the ecosystem is to develop and ratify standards. Certification, based on training and assessment, is an example of this. Higher-qualified members of an ecosystem are then allowed to take on more complex or higher-value projects. They can be ranked as 'Tier 1' suppliers, for example. The cooperative nature of business ecosystems also encourages informal methods of improvement through knowledge transfer and the development of communities to share knowledge and experience on common technical issues.

In many market sectors, the business ecosystem has replaced traditional relationships of buyers and sellers with communities of interacting organisations that together create, deliver and consume goods and services. These relationships should evolve in response to changes in the business environment, market conditions and the specific initiatives of individual members. Slowly-changing, rigid supply chains are being replaced by more fluid, flexible structures based on alliances, partnerships and collaborations. This model offers both small and large companies opportunities to grow through cooperation and evolution.

To get full benefit from a business ecosystem, you need to manage your involvement in the same way as you manage partnerships. That means identifying the right mix of partners, setting up and managing the relationships and ensuring that the infrastructure supports effective collaborative working. As a member of a business ecosystem, you can offer your own customers a wider range of services and solutions, strengthening your own marketing capability.

Take your partners ...

Partnership is now an integral part of an effective business strategy. Companies are no longer embarrassed about the fact that they work with other people and don't do everything themselves. A strong list of partners and the ability to manage an ecosystem are now seen as important factors in the buying decision. Partnership enables you to build on your core strengths and use the skills and resources of other companies to fill the gaps or open new opportunities for your business. But for partnership to succeed, you have to work hard at managing the process and make sure all parties benefit.

The benefits of partnership, like the benefits of any other marketing programme, should be measurable, as the final chapter explains.

16

Measure for measure – just what is marketing success?

THROUGHOUT THIS BOOK, we've let you into some great secrets. Now you can use them to build and enhance your position. Put them into practice and you could make a real impact on your company's success and your own career prospects.

That's vital because, in the cost-cutting environment that followed the onset of the recent economic recession, boards are looking hard at the performance and contribution of every department. Okay, it's clear things have moved on from the days when John Wanamaker said, 'Half the money I spend on advertising is wasted – the trouble is I don't know which half'. But now the emphasis is firmly on measurement and boards are demanding a greater return on marketing investment. Follow the guidelines you've learnt in this book and you'll have the tools – and the results – to deliver that return and demonstrate direct bottom-line responsibility.

Implementing the marketing secrets in this book will put you in the driving seat in three key areas:

1   Marketing will get the respect it deserves in your company.

2   You'll get the budget you need to meet your objectives.

3   The board will recognise that marketing makes money rather than takes it.

Marketing secret

◆   When you can measure the results of what you do, you'll find it easier to justify the resources and budgets you need.

Sure, your creative marketing activities raise awareness and get the company noticed, but when your colleagues under-stand how you help to build profitable

understand the overall business objectives

long-term business, that's when you gain the real respect. Your role becomes more business-focused and aligned with higher-level objectives. You demonstrate that you understand the overall business objectives and that you are in tune with what your business needs and what it wants to achieve. That makes you a vital player.

Make a commercial impact

So, how do you demonstrate a measurable return to your company? The return can be direct, in terms of revenue and profit contribution, or indirect, in terms of improved cus-tomer satisfaction or shareholder value. Marketing success can be measured in many different ways, but it's important to present your results in terms of return on investment because that's the language financial controllers and board members speak. These are just a few examples:

◆ Customer retention programmes translate directly into bottom-line performance over the long term. As we showed in Chapter 2, long-term customer relationships create greater lifetime value, and it costs less to service existing customers, compared to recruiting new ones.

◆ Partner recruitment programmes can add real value to your company's capability. With the right partners, your company can build additional revenue streams from new products or new markets. Partnership can also reduce costs by focusing on core activities and outsourcing to specialists.

◆ Marketing campaigns and communications that nurture leads have a major influence on the complex, lengthy purchase cycles that are increasingly common, particularly in business-to-business markets. That means you can reduce the time to revenue and cut the costs of doing business.

◆ Brand differentiation can create a vital competitive advantage that underpins all the other sales and marketing processes. That way you can make it easier to increase revenue and retain business over the long term.

The four examples above all make an important contribution to costs, revenue and profit, demonstrating that your activities make a positive return on marketing investment and add real value to the business.

> *Marketing secret*
>
> ◆ The real measure of marketing success is not today's great campaign, it's the contribution to building profitable long-term business.

Using the marketing secrets in this book, you can show:

◆ your marketing investment is driving the most sales and profits in the short term, and maximising longer-term financial value

◆ you're using marketing expenditure wisely by measuring the revenue impact of campaigns and relating every sale to the original marketing campaign source

◆ you're using marketing resources to the short- and long-term benefit of your company by measuring the impact and return on marketing investment

◆ you're making specific, measurable returns from marketing expenditure and focusing marketing budgets on the activities that generate the most revenue.

Measurement can change marketing direction

Here's an example of how that can work in practice. A computer manufacturer was considering a controversial marketing communications programme for its service division. Traditionally, the company's sales and marketing focus was on hardware because that's where the main revenue stream came from. To smooth the way for hardware sales, the company's account managers frequently offered services like planning, design and installation to customers at no charge. Internally, those services were treated as a cost of sales.

However, a new marketing director with a background in services argued that the company would derive greater financial and customer retention benefits from turning those services into chargeable items. This was based on the fact that many customers struggled with product installation and maintenance using their own support teams. As a result, there was a poor perception of the company's products, satisfaction levels were low and account losses high.

When the marketing director requested funds to communicate the new service offer to customers, there was considerable opposition and scepticism from both the board and the sales and product management teams. Fortunately, the board decided to trust his judgement, but set demanding objectives and financial targets. The communications programme succeeded and, within a year, marketing metrics showed that revenue from services had overtaken hardware sales and customer satisfaction levels had increased significantly. In the longer term, customer retention levels increased. That was a very clear return on marketing investment.

Measure outcomes, not activities

Marketing measurement like that described above enables you to analyse and improve the efficiency and effectiveness of your marketing by aligning marketing activities, strategies and metrics with your company's business goals. It's easy to concentrate on activity-based measures such as tracking

*focus on the business
outcomes of your
campaigns and
programmes*

downloads, numbers of website visitors, campaign responses or event attendance levels. However, the most effective types of marketing measurement focus on the business outcomes of your campaigns and programmes, such as share of market, rate of customer acquisition, average order value, rate of new product and service adoptions, growth in customer buying frequency, volume and share of business, customer loyalty levels, and rate of growth compared to competition.

> *Marketing secret*
>
> ◆ Measuring activities is important; measuring outcomes demonstrates your real value to the business.

In the example of the computer company services programme above, the campaign ticked all those boxes. It succeeded in the eyes of the board because the campaign worked within the framework of clear, measurable objectives. Measurements such as these help management boards to recognise that marketing is a necessary investment for generating and maintaining profit, rather than just a cost or expense. It's clear that getting the right measurements in place is central to marketing success. It doesn't just tell you how you are doing, it gives you the ammunition to justify your requests for marketing budget and resources. So whenever you apply the secrets of success from this book, make sure you identify the potential business benefits and measure them.

What's the real measure of success?

Remember that the people who are most important to your business are your customers and the real measure of success is their lifetime value. Keep the customer satisfied and you've got a source of income and profit that will keep building. The key to satisfaction is treating each customer as an individual, understanding their needs and building a personalised service that makes them recognise the value of your company. The real measure of your success is not the quarterly results but the value you build over the long term. So, remember, you're in for the long haul. You've got great brands to grow, reputations to build and customer satisfaction to maintain. You can do that by making your budgets work harder and bringing the whole company on board. Great marketing doesn't just happen in isolation, it takes everyone in the company to play their role in satisfying the customer. It's a great challenge, but follow the secrets of success in this book and you've made a fantastic start.

Index

delivery
  resourcing's emphasis on 223
Dell 47, 55
departmental managers 156,
  212
direct mail 6, 186
direct response advertising 157
discounting 129–30, 140
discussion group, online 45,
  218

e-marketing 230–1
economy pricing 139
employees
  and informal innovation
    networks 39–40
  and internal marketing
    212–14
entertainment venues
  and smartcards 15–16
events
  and resourcing 228
  sponsorship of 118–19
executive briefing meetings 118
exhibitions 185
extranets 243

'fast-fit' car repairs 106, 107
feedback, customer *see* customer
  feedback
finance, offering to customers
  109–12
finance executives 154
financial controls 171
financial stability 165–6
first-class pricing 139
forums *see* customer forums,
  online

'Hall of Fame' 45–6
hidden communicators,
  empowering 211–14

high cost-to-serve customers
  29–30

implementation services 108–9
industry surveys 157
informal innovation networks
  39–41
innovation
  and business ecosystems
    250–2
  creating a culture of 215–17
  creating a stronger culture of
    through partnership 237
  distinction between invention
    and 215
  importance of 215
  and informal networks 39–41
innovation community, building
  217–19
innovation showcase 44
integrated marketing 179–93
  consistency of messages 182–
    3, 196
  contribution to greater
    marketing precision 186
  and corporate identity 183
  and creative integrity 180–2,
    190
  hi-fi system campaign
    example 190–3
  indicators demonstrating
    need for 180
  and operational efficiency
    187–8
  and reduction of marketing
    costs 189–90
  unbiased media
    recommendations 183–5
  use of database marketing
    techniques 186
  use of different media 184–5